I0753242

ALGORITHM

IMAGE

ART

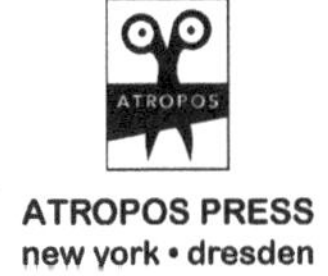

ATROPOS PRESS
new york • dresden

ALGORITHM IMAGE ART

ROSEMARY LEE

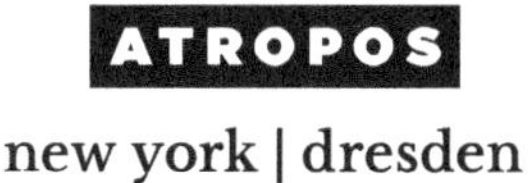

ATROPOS PRESS
NEW YORK | DRESDEN

THINK MEDIA SERIES IS SUPPORTED BY THE EUROPEAN GRADUATE SCHOOL

ATROPOS PRESS
151 FIRST AVENUE # 14, NEW YORK, N.Y. 10003
MOCKRITZER STR. 6, D-01219, DRESDEN, GERMANY

COVER DESIGN BY: DAVID CRIXEL
BOOK INTERIOR DESIGN BY: MILENE NEY

ISBN: 978-1-7375591-4-6

TABLE OF CONTENTS

INTRODUCTION

Algorithms play an increasingly influential role in the production, circulation, and interpretation of images, a shift that has complex implications for art, the humanities, and visual culture. Machine learning has become pervasive beyond the technical research contexts it emerged from and had previously been largely confined to, finding a wide variety of visual applications from the direct generation of images to influencing the display of visual content based on the large-scale collection and analysis of data. The highly automated performance of visual processing tasks by machines allows digital aesthetics to be informed by algorithms, statistical models and data. As a result, images are increasingly defined by their engagement with algorithms, which structure them aesthetically, processually, and semantically in ways that often exceed description in terms of direct human perception, agency, and understanding, while being to a great extent informed by and entangled with these. In this sense, recent technical developments such as the computational generation of images using machine learning systems tap into long-running theoretical challenges regarding the non-visual, immaterial, and non-human aspects of art, images, and visual media. This book examines how the algorithmic structuring of images may offer new ways of understanding recent technical developments and their surrounding discourses. Through close examination of relevant instances from the history of visual technologies, we consider how current discourses surrounding nascent forms of image-making may in some cases disrupt while in others reinforcing established conventions in thinking about visual media.

Visual technologies that emphasize algorithms, statistical models, and data reshape not only the way images appear but also how they behave and what significance they have. While they may be nearly ubiquitous, algorithms often play a cryptic role in visual media, creating a distinct gap between the visible surface of an image and processes and data behind. We may understand the recent predominance of machine learning as a paradigm image-making as an *algorithmic turn* in visual media (Ulricchio, 2011), prioritizing data and the performance of algorithmic processes over the visual qualities of what is output by a given system. In combination with a high degree of technical opacity, this throws the complex relationships between the visual and nonvisual aspects of algorithmic forms of imaging into contention with traditional perspectives that assume a close referential correspondence between images and real-world phenomena.

The growing technical capacities of algorithmic visual media have attracted the attention of artists, theorists, and institutions curious to understand what implications this may have for art, visual media, society, and digital culture, which has resulted in a wave of practical experimentation and theoretical inquiry on this topic. Artists', theorists', and artist-theorists' explorations have yielded new ways of thinking about images, visual media, and the cultural role of technology, with contributions taking the form of art projects, technical experiments, and theoretical texts approaching from various perspectives. Critically-engaged discussions on machine learning have pointed out ethically problematic assumptions, internal logic, and extractivist tendencies embedded in the very foundations of the procurement, management, and implementation of data-based approaches to visual media.

The development of machine learning tools that are accessible to non-experts has given machine learning and *artificial intelligence* (AI) widespread use and visibility in the general public. One effect this has is that it enables users to create images in new ways than had been possible previously without significant technical knowledge, to some extent domesticating the technology, but also in some cases revealing its limitations in terms of technical capacities, the tendency towards difficult to remediate error and bias, and conceptual framings that often reiterate existing clichés such as robot apocalypse or AIs as artists. While the recent popularity of intersections between AI and art has become a lively sphere for experimentation and discussion, many aspects continue to pose significant theoretical challenges. A contributing factor to difficulties in critically grappling with this area of research is that the processes that go on within machine learning systems are often opaque to human understanding, even to those who design, build, and operate them. Rapidly growing technical affordances, corporations' active attempts to conceal the inner workings of their technologies, and the ideas attached to the term *artificial intelligence* have a tendency to obscure what is at stake in the use of highly automated visual systems to create and interpret images.

Certain conceptual ambiguities emerge from machine learning's historical association with artificial intelligence. This includes a recurring reliance on cybernetic metaphors, drawing comparisons between biological and ecological systems to the modalities at work in technical systems. Likening computers to human brains can indeed help to illustrate how the tasks performed by machines may share related attributes with cognition, reasoning, and intelligence. But such analogies often lend themselves more to opacity than clarity, contributing to inaccuracies as well as reinforcing dangerous biases within technical systems. Beyond the misconceptions that machine learning brings with it, there is also a long history of skepticism towards the use of new technologies in art, often centered on familiar themes such as the threat they may pose to the role of the (human) author, or a reversal on this premise, treating the machine as an artist or author.

In attempting to grapple with novel aspects in contemporary art and visual media that have resulted from the pervasive influence of algorithms, we are confronted with existing conventions in thinking about images that have accompanied nascent visual technologies in the past. Current forms of visual media may in some respects depart from older paradigms, for example by affording new levels of acceleration, automation, and introducing new modalities into both the creation and interpretation of visual content. Yet the images generated by machine learning systems are not entirely distinct from other visual paradigms, allowing a heterogeneity of image paradigms to coexist across a range of different media. And, importantly, algorithmic qualities, processes, and structural influences can be found even in much earlier time periods than the contexts we are most familiar with today.

Recent developments contribute to the emergence of new perspectives that often defy traditional conceptions of images. In contrast to defining images as primarily visual, materially individuated objects, whose value derives from the investment of human labor and intellect, media artifacts are increasingly understood as processual, ontologically ambiguous, and governed by programmed machines. These qualities and the historical threads that they draw upon are far from linear, disrupting conceptions of the history of technology as a flow of successive developments and rather affording a heterogeneity of different attributes, imaging paradigms, and conceptual associations to coexist within a single image.

The progression from the use of relatively simple algorithmic methods to structure the visual composition of an image towards the more complex, automated, and artificially creative systems that are commonplace today has taken place through diverse and often seemingly unconnected instances across a span of many centuries. Approaching the topic of algorithmic visual media from this perspective enables us to find commonalities between recent approaches and diverse examples such as the execution of images through the systematic use of pre-defined sets of written instructions, geometry, optics, or mechanical automation that have in various ways led up to or informed the present context. In such cases, algorithmic techniques may be performed by hand or using simple technical apparatus in place of the highly automated processes that are now performed by digital computers, but the underlying principles and modalities employed bear resemblances to one another that may offer insights into current artifacts, practices, and ideas.

While the role of technology in image-making and in art has been extensively discussed, it remains an area in which there is little consensus, even on foundational issues such as answering the seemingly simple question "What is an image?" notably problematized by W. J. T. Mitchell (1986). Images, algorithms, and art each entail a philosophical slipperiness in their own right, often proving more easily identified than they are to define. Images — as algorithms and art — are transmedial, transcending beyond instantiation in any particular, material form, something that is emphasized in their performance according to algorithmic constraints and procedures. This adds to the existing difficulty of developing coherent image ontologies, as it problematizes attempts at clearly defining what an image is, or what it is not, for that matter. The ephemeral nature of images also challenges us to find similarities in modality across what may be at least superficially diverse forms of media and approaches to image-making in a way that cuts against the grain of conventions that tend to segment visual culture according to linear chronologies, taxonomies of media, and disciplinary divisions.

This work seeks to unpack the interrelations of algorithms, images, and art. Drawing from the perspectives of art history and media archaeology, it builds upon the central insights developed during the course of my Ph.D. research *Machine Learning and Notions of the Image* (Lee, 2020). Considering how notions of the image have been influenced by the rise of machine learning as an imaging paradigm, I seek to situate current discussions of algorithmic media in relation to relevant historical tendencies that have greatly shaped not only visual technologies, but also importantly, how ideas about those developments have become embedded in ongoing discourse. Contextualizing recent technical developments in relation to relevant cultural precursors across a great expanse of time has the consequence of sacrificing depth in the interest of breadth. Rather than attempting to develop an exhaustive account of this topic, the goal of this investigation is to probe interconnections within this rather complex tangle of how algorithms change but also express and respond to various aspects of culture. This, I find, is at once a limitation of my own research but also where I call upon others to continue building upon it. Seeking to ground the ongoing discussions that already surround the image and its intersections with technologies and art, we look at the images, structures, data, processes, and histories behind algorithmically-produced images.

While this exploration explicitly focuses on topics within art and art history, it actively seeks to touch on the ideas behind, in and associated with technologies of visualization and how they have developed over time, more so than focusing solely on their particular instantiation. This is not to say that current methods will soon lose their relevance due to the rapid pace at which technologies and the discourses around them change. Rather, by examining how tendencies have developed over time, we may draw insights into what ways they may progress in the future. Another reason for focusing mostly on art historical examples is that this book aims to provide a roadmap of sorts that can be of use to future research and artistic practice. I believe that art cannot be made while limited solely to thinking about art and find that often conceptual infrastructure is of greater use than the sole analysis of particular, contemporary instances.

This investigation of the intersections of algorithms, images, and art seeks to dig into aspects of the history of ideas that are under-recognized in contemporary discourse. And while this work has emerged from research specifically into the use of machine learning in contemporary art, it also encourages readers to reflect on the contexts and narratives surrounding technologically engaged art and media artifacts, more so than fixating on any one particular technology, approach, or visual paradigm in itself.

Algorithmic forms of visual media cut across a variety of different media from diverse time periods. This holds vital implications for contemporary contexts in which algorithmic approaches such as machine learning and artificial intelligence, in general, have become extremely influential in image-making as well as how developments in these fields are theorized. Considering this phenomenon in terms of its significance to art contexts offers a view of contemporary practices that engage critically in what cultural significance algorithmic visual media may have, now as well as in the future. Comparing current ideas and methods to those of the past not only grounds this study in relation to the long history of algorithmic media, but also compels us to question certain assumptions that have become deeply engrained in contexts surrounding art, technology, and conceptions of the image.

This research engages questions about the role of technology in the production of images and art, while also touching on a number of interrelated issues, including the mediation of perception that occurs through images, the automation of production processes, and how visual culture may be read differently as a result of these. Algorithms ultimately have a structuring influence, aesthetically, processually, and as a result, conceptually, on the image. Organizing the performance of image-making processes according to pre-defined constraints has several effects, including enabling the production of images to be guided by a formal set of instructions and rules. This, in turn, facilitates the storage, transmission, repeatability, and iterability of the algorithmic image, contributing not only to the proliferation of images but also allowing a degree of consistency to be maintained within serially produced images.

Another key feature of algorithmic image-making is that it lends itself to automation, enabling machines to be programmed to perform or execute algorithmic procedures in place of humans. Shifting perspectives on relationships between the technical mediation of human vision, images, and real-world phenomena have led to an increasing emphasis on images as both a form of and based on visual data. This ultimately throws the empirical basis of data-based images into contention, something that has also been considered in discussions around earlier technological paradigms of image-making than those of today. The adoption of advanced visual technologies in artistic practices also raises difficult to remediate issues concerning the extent to which technical affordances of these systems and their embedded biases, limitations, and worldviews are challenged or rather perpetuated in such strategies of appropriation.

The image acts as an interface between the visual and the non-visual, between human and machinic intentionality, and between making and interpreting images. These various points of flexion are made especially apparent in the modalities of forms of media that employ machine learning, exploring the malleability of the boundaries between visual and non-visual, between human and machine, and between the processes entailed in the production of images and their interpretation. In order to reflect the nuanced nature of its topic, this book adopts a fairly non-linear approach, exploring intricate webs of association between technical processes and modalities in image production and their surrounding discourses. Each chapter seeks to address a slice of the issues connected with this topic from a different angle rather than progressing in strictly chronological order. Pulling at constituent threads, we unravel some of the entanglement of image, non-image, art and not art, human and machine, and vision and process.

Chapter 1, *Algorithmic Image Production,* introduces the topic of the recent tendency towards the increasing use of algorithmic methods such as machine learning in image production. It describes how the generation of images using machine learning has come to occupy the interest of theorists and practitioners across multiple fields including contemporary art, media studies, and computer science and it presents the premise that recent technical developments in the production of images draw on discourse from the history of art and visual media, as well as theories of the image.

In Chapter 2, *Approximation,* we begin by looking at analog forms of algorithmic image-making methods that facilitate an understanding of similar processes at work in the highly automated systems in use today. As a starting point, we examine an ancient method of cartography that enabled the transcription of maps in written form and several other examples in which textual instructions for the production of images were formulated in terms of geometric, proportional relationships. Considering this example through the concept of the *softimage* (Hoelzl and Marie, 2015), we consider how approaches to image-making based on the implementation of simple, analog sets of instructions set the stage for thinking about significant aspects in contemporary forms of algorithmic image-making. This opens up several interrelated threads that are picked up in subsequent chapters, looking at how algorithmic approaches may contribute to images' capacity for latency, automation by machines, and the embedding of optical relationships within the image plane.

The following chapter, *Transcription,* discusses how the transcodability of images into alphanumeric form structures the process of image-making and endows them with the quality of transmediality. Creating images according to sets of algorithmic instructions enables them to exist in latent, unarticulated, form, to be reproduced, or to be iterated upon, and to exist across a range of media, aspects that hold implications for assessments of the cultural and economic value of images as cultural products, but also for the challenge of establishing image ontologies. Through *procedural practices* (Carvalhais, 2016) and the *dematerialization of the art object* (Lippard, 1973) in conceptual art, we discuss how an understanding of the processes involved in the production of a work of art — or an image — came to be seen as contributing to one's evaluation of cultural artifacts.

Chapter 4, *Automation,* discusses how technological developments have given rise to a reckoning with the value of human labor that may be displaced by the automation of image production. An emphasis on process has been significant to the use of procedural methods in movements such as Surrealist automatism, and how these contributed to the early development of generative strategies in art. This leads us to consider how ideas about relationships between human and machine visual interpretation and expressions of agency have been powerful factors in value judgments in art, images, and visual media, in general.

Chapter 5, *Alignment,* looks at the positioning of the human point of view relative to images. First it examines early methodologies and apparatuses for the incorporation of optical principles into the production of images in forms of what Friedrich Kittler refers to as *optical media* (1999). It then considers the optical paradigm in terms of the idea of the image as an accurate reflection of the world and what implications this has for understandings of the mediation of perception that occurs through technological forms of image-making.

The following chapter, *Operation,* delves further into the tension between the visual and the processual aspects of images which arises from the algorithmic formulation of images. We look into this through Harun Farocki's *operational image* (2004) and several other related theories concerning the visual, non-visual, and processual aspects of images. Through this concept, we examine the idea of the image as something that is enacted and acts on the world, rather than strictly representing it.

In Chapter 7, *Refraction,* we look at several historical examples in which composite images are made through the combination of multiple individual images. Here we consider parallels between the use of such an approach and the complex processes involved in machine learning systems. This again raises the issue of treating images and data as interchangeable. On the one hand, such instances often entail associations between technical and scientific methods and presumed degrees of inherent truthfulness that result from their application in image-making, while on the other, the synthesis performed in producing composite images often plays a significant role in shaping the results. Considering this through historical discourse on photographic media and through Lorraine Daston and Peter Galison's (2007) work on various forms of visual objectivity in scientific imaging, we explore a range of different perspectives on the mediating role of technical forms of visual representation.

The concluding chapter, *Distortion,* examines how the automation of visual processing tasks may inform the interpretation of the resulting images. Drawing on the potential for divergence between visual aesthetics of images and the data and processes that lie "behind" or "below" the visible, we discuss how situations of error enable us to see otherwise invisible aspects of visual media.

ALGORITHMIC IMAGE PRODUCTION

Images are increasingly informed by their engagement with algorithms, with the growing ubiquity, but also processing power of machine learning giving rise to the proliferation of new practices, aesthetics, and theories in image-making, art, and visual culture at large. The effects of algorithms on images have a tendency to subvert existing theoretical conventions, as they are connected to highly automated and dynamic processes in ways that not always clear. Characterizing images, art, and visual media as "algorithmic" emphasizes that these may be defined to a greater extent by their procedural qualities than their position relative to human perceptual experience and expressions of agency. In this sense, recent developments in the technical production of images present certain aspects of genuine novelty, challenging traditional evaluation criteria that have typically prioritized visual aesthetics, human authorship, and direct referential forms of representation, yet they are often accompanied by narratives that originally emerged in relation to earlier visual paradigms such as photography, painting, or drawing. Examining how current examples, methods, and contexts are informed by historical tendencies in visual technologies and their surrounding discourses, this investigation focuses on the theoretical and artistic implications of algorithmic methods and machine learning. By situating recent developments in the use of machine learning to produce images in relation to instances drawn from the history of art and of visual media, it seeks to develop a better understanding of the historical threads that converge in the use of algorithmic approaches in recent artistic practice.

An *algorithm* can be explained as a recipe of sorts, or "a set of modular or autonomous instructions — in execution — for the doing or making of something, which includes necessary elements, constraints and procedure, taken together dynamically" (Bianco, 2018, p. 24). When generating an image using a machine learning system, the algorithm is the sequence of operations performed by a computer in solving a given problem. In this case, the "problem" may be framed as a question of how to create an image that reflects the attributes of a given dataset. It's important to note that, contrary to a popular misconception, it is not the algorithm that changes over time, but the model. The algorithm is performed, often repeatedly, and a statistical model is updated and adjusted to improve the performance of the algorithm at a given task. A trained machine learning model, therefore, comes to bear the impressions of the content and context to which it is applied.

Melanie Mitchell defines *machine learning* as "a subfield of artificial intelligence (AI) in which machines 'learn' from data or from their own 'experiences'" (2019, p. 8). In such an approach, a statistical model is "trained" or adjusted in relation to the relative success or accuracy of its output, aimed at improving the performance of an algorithm at a given task over time. This enables visual processing tasks such as the generation, classification, or labeling of images, to be performed by highly automated computer systems. Mitchell situates machine learning within artificial intelligence, which she describes as "a branch of computer science that studies the properties of intelligence by synthesizing intelligence" (p. 7). While rather recursive, this definition gives us a starting point to work from and illustrates this topic's potential for ambiguities.

It's historically significant that the term *artificial intelligence* was coined with the explicit intention of establishing a new direction from cybernetics research, from which it and machine learning emerged. *Cybernetics* draws inspiration from biological and environmental feedback systems in the design of technical systems. For example, by modeling human cognition or biological vision in computational systems, parallels between various kinds of processes could drive new forms of technological development. Remnants of this history are invoked by the use of artificial intelligence as a marketing tool and in cultural metaphors that draw cybernetic comparisons between human brains and programmed machines. Such instances frequently rely on misconceptions regarding the nature of intelligence and technical attempts at replicating it, computationally, as well as having the potential to distract from the realities of what is truly at stake in AI.

This area of research has developed rapidly in the past 10 years, with artists often keen to be first-adopters of emerging technical affordances as they are developed. As a result, machine learning has been implemented in an increasingly broad range of visual applications beyond its prior limits within computer science research. From the direct generation of images to determining the visibility of networked content, machine learning has become pervasive in many tools and forms of visual media that are accessible to non-experts. Algorithmic processes have thereby come to have a pervasive influence on visual media, as well as cultural imaginaries surrounding this tendency.

In combination with the growing technical potential of machine learning the conceptual associations attached to artificial intelligence and the performance of algorithms have proven especially relevant in art contexts. In recent years, this has resulted in a growing number of exhibitions, funding opportunities, research projects, and even the establishment of labs dedicated to the topic of *AI art* (Zylinska, 2020). The wide-ranging technical, theoretical, and societal implications of machine learning and artificial intelligence have drawn the interest of high-profile artists who have worked with machine learning, both thematically and from a technical standpoint. Theorists have also weighed in on this topic, providing philosophical insights and often working closely with practitioners across several fields. It is a great challenge to select which examples to focus on, as those discussed here are just a few of the growing number of practitioners and thinkers who have made significant artistic and theoretical contributions relevant to this topic.

There are various ways of incorporating machine learning in visual art, among which image generator systems have become especially widespread. Generative adversarial networks (GANs), introduced in 2014, became a popular machine learning approach among artists for the relatively high-quality, photographic images they generate. Since early 2022, GANs have been largely overshadowed by diffusion models. Several popular examples of this kind of image generator system include DALL-E 2, Midjourney, or Stable Diffusion, which have recently experienced widespread media coverage in the general public for their ability to create images with photographic aesthetics from input text prompts. These shifting tendencies have been encouraged by a number of factors including new technical developments, growing accessibility to the technology and knowledge of how to use it, as well as increasing the cultural visibility of artificial intelligence.

In the context of image production, machine learning enables images to be informed by the application of statistical models so that new visual content may be generated based on the analysis of a dataset. Recent developments in machine learning research for graphical applications have afforded new ways of creating and analyzing images. A statistical model is said to be "trained" on a dataset, from which the system "learns" or extracts patterns that in turn inform adjustments to the model with the aim of improving its performance. There are various ways of doing this, but one common practice is for machine learning datasets to be composed of examples fitting the attributes desired to be learned.

Beyond directly shaping visual content, machine learning is frequently integrated into other software, where its influence is often obscure to users. Digital cameras and many apps may automatically detect faces, gestures, or facial expressions, adjust lighting and focus, or add a filter or lens in real-time as photographs are taken. Machine learning has also become ubiquitous in networked contexts, where it is unclear what criteria are entailed in determining the visibility of online content. The opacity of the algorithmic processes behind many forms of visual media contributes to ambiguity in mainstream understandings of what algorithms are and what role they play in digital media.

Training a model relies on providing a machine learning system with suitable data, usually meaning an ample amount of data that is of high quality and fits a specific scope. What high-quality means, in this case, is quite open to interpretation and the quantity and kind of data required to successfully train a machine learning model are also variable, although it's generally agreed that the more data there is and the more representative it is of the phenomenon in consideration, the greater likelihood there is of achieving the intended results. But as has been duly pointed out, the express intentions behind a machine learning application may have little to do with the actual outcomes that result from such unpredictable processes.

This touches on the problem of measuring the accuracy of visual media, which is especially problematic in the case of machine learning systems that persistently prove prone to embedded bias and error, and are open to variation based on the parameters, data, methods, and contexts involved. On the one hand, machine learning systems have demonstrated a capacity to achieve statistically unpredictable results. But it has become clear in recent years that one thing that is not unpredictable in machine learning is its tendency towards highly problematic instances of built-in bias that originate in the human perspectives that have informed the design, application, and evaluation of machine learning systems.

Although algorithms are in themselves clearly defined and deterministic, the results of applying them to the production of images entails various potential openings for ambiguity. There may be substantial differences between the way that the visual qualities of an image or the processes involved in its production are perceived and understood by humans in comparison to the way the same image may be interpreted by a computer. Variations between the particularities of a given system, as opposed to another, may also radically impact the results of automating a visual processing task. The outputs of machine learning systems are far from self-evident, often requiring specific knowledge or external information in order to be "read" or understood on more than a superficial level. Aspects of machine learning, such as the fact that different results may be achieved each time a given operation is performed, make its results difficult to predict, meaning that these systems and their outputs can be opaque to human understanding. While this may, on the one hand, allow them to deliver surprising results, it again raises the issue of the limits of human perspectives on algorithmic media on the level of design, implementation, and assessment of their outputs.

Creating images in accordance with clearly defined constraints and procedures serves as a starting point from which to discuss relationships between recent developments in machine learning and aspects of earlier forms of image-making technologies. Images may be transcribed as — or enacted from — written instructions outlining the specifics of how an image is to be produced. Algorithmic sets of instructions may be used to produce several different iterations of the same image that are constrained by pre-defined rules. This enables a degree of unity to be maintained between several instantiations, as well as affording the transcription of instructions for the creation of an image in written form, like a program for its execution. These aspects raise several challenges to the development of image ontologies and the evaluation of art, issues that become especially visible in the highly automated and networked contexts in which algorithmic media are ubiquitous today.

The increasing formulation of images in terms of algorithmic processes draws attention to the act of imaging as an event, a mode of committing to memory, of making a spatial experience perceptible and communicable. In this light, it becomes understandable why one might photograph something without any intention of looking at that image, itself, again. The act of capturing the moment, of participating in its orchestration and archival, outweighs the image as a visual record. More than visually documenting objects, ideas, and contexts, producing images allows us to form a particular relation to the visual. The conditions surrounding an image's performance and articulation correspondingly also inform its reception, making it a site of mediation between human perception, meaning making, and agency, also demanding new forms of technical literacy to interpret the products of highly automated algorithmic systems.

The widespread adoption of machine learning in a variety of different fields emerges from a long history in which conflicting perspectives on visual technologies have shaped thinking about images. In the history of photography, for example, the application of technical processes and apparatuses has been demonstrated to have the capacity to produce highly accurate visual representations, while also being open to the manipulation of appearances. Mechanical automation and later the increasingly computational nature of visual media enabled production processes to be made increasingly programmatic, with implications for evaluating the products of highly automated machines, not only in terms of their own characteristics, but also in terms of other factors such as their position relative to human perception, interpretation, and agency. Data-intensive approaches to image-making such as machine learning in many ways expand on, rather than distinctly departing from these narratives, and thus highlight existing ambiguities in image studies concerning not only the defining qualities of images but also how their meaning is constructed.

The recent popularity of algorithmic methods has been characterized by William Ulricchio (2011) as an *algorithmic turn* that departs in certain respects from prior conceptualizations of images and visual media. Rather than irrevocably breaking from them, this shift expands on tendencies present in image production, even in much older, analog practices. While machine learning offers new ways of creating and interpreting images, it does not make a complete break from earlier technical and visual paradigms of image-making. Instead, it often draws on elements derived from a variety of different forms of visual media. For example, images generated using machine learning often have what may be considered a *photographic* appearance, both in the sense of applying a particular realistic visual aesthetic as well as entailing processual connotations inherited from analog photography. This two-fold character draws on conceptions of the image as at once a visual representation of the world, as in the tradition of photography, and the product of a database (Hoelzl and Marie, 2015), which in machine learning often entails being directly derived from a database composed of digital photographs.

Recent technical developments in visual media have given rise to discussions of the "changing ontology of the image" (Lund, 2021) in the sense that the modalities of algorithmic processes often subvert traditional expectations of what defines an image. As Harun Farocki (2004) points out, highly automated forms of images may be operative in the sense that they "do not represent an object, but rather are part of an operation" (p. 17). In this way, the use of algorithms in image-making emphasizes processual qualities and the interpretation of data over conceptions of images as materially fixed, visual likenesses of real-world objects.

The generation of images based on learned patterns in datasets disrupts the apparent direct visual referential connection between image and the world that is found in other forms of image-making. A generated digital image's pixel values may be determined by statistical patterns in data that have little to do with how it is interpreted by human viewers. The incorporation of machine learning into the production of images thereby adds to an already complex area of discourse surrounding the technologically mediated nature of image-making, being at once highly technical and based on data while open to ambiguity and error. Visual technologies tend to be viewed as offering a level of scientific accuracy in that act of representation, creating referential connections between the image and the things or ideas it is intended to point to or stand in for. This is especially noticeable in the history of photography, where technical apparatus and process play a significant role in mediating the referentiality of the images that are produced in this fashion, and because of this, there is a tendency to assume that images that appear photographic or that employ technical processes like those of photography imply stable relationships between visual representations and their referents.

The growing technical promise, ubiquity, and cultural implications of algorithmic approaches to image production draw together multiple, overlapping value systems and traditions surrounding images, especially those at the convergence of art and technology. But while this may appear to be a new phenomenon, structuring the production of images according to defined sets of rules, calculations, data, or constraints is not exclusive to the digital forms that are currently predominant. Many aspects of even much older techniques and technologies of image-making than those involving machine learning or even digital technology have become embedded in the invisible infrastructure behind algorithmic visual media. This includes the value systems that color the experience, interpretation, and assessment of images, that have been shaped by earlier visual traditions such as those that have been built up around photography, painting, and drawing.

In *The Finiteness of Algorithms*, Friedrich Kittler (2007) traces the origin of the word "algorithm" back to the corruption of the name Muhammad ibn Mūsā al-Khwārizmī through its successive interpretation, articulation, and reinterpretation. In so doing, Kittler points not only to the long, non-linear history of algorithms, but also to the fact that it mirrors the very qualities of algorithms, themselves: culturally programmed, reiterated, and decoded ad libitum.

We have algorithms and processes on one side, and artworks on the other side, and between them things like the camera obscura, the Turing machine, computers, and more basic things: palettes, painting tools, and musical instruments. Things within which knowledge, often thousands of years of knowledge, have accumulated, knowledge that is, however, different from that which is in artworks; instruments and machines collect knowledge in order to create works and processes. (Kittler, 2007)

Images, algorithms, and art transcend beyond any individual material instantiation in ways that defy attempts at pinning them down. They also share a complex, intertwined history that engages a number of largely unresolved issues across several intersecting fields. In terms of methods, apparatus, as well as the ideas associated with them, early precursor technologies to those that are currently prevalent have influenced thinking about visual media in formative ways. Prior to the development of the computational methods that are now employed in visual media, related ideas, and modalities have either influenced or offer insights into the present context. Image-making has had a longstanding entanglement with algorithms, albeit often taking on forms that are unfamiliar but that are nevertheless relevant today.

The history of algorithmic visual media is much longer than those instances involving the use of digital computers. Analog algorithmic processes have been employed in image-making and in art for a very long time and while they are especially prevalent now, accelerated with the aid of automation, digital computation, and machine learning, algorithmic media is distinct from any particular technology it may be articulated through. Examples from this history offer insight into several aspects of current forms of algorithmic media that are often highly opaque to intuitive understanding. Drawing connections to distant precursors to today's use of algorithms in visual contexts also allows us to delve into some of the historical value judgments that have accompanied imaging technologies, and that persistently haunt discourse on visual media.

Examining the deep history behind the use of machine learning in visual media, the following chapters consider the accumulated knowledge that has become embedded in the technical production of images. The view of images as the product of data holds resounding implications for many different aspects of visual media. This tendency has reshaped the way that we make sense of the world around us, directly in terms of human visual perception. It also has deeper relevance to the way we make sense out of that which is perceived, as advanced visual technologies change how we think about what we see. Examining these themes through historical examples in the following chapters, we build toward the examination of how ideas built up around visual technologies contribute to current narratives surrounding machine learning.

APPROXIMATION

Though it may be an unlikely place to look for insights into the topic of algorithmic media, an atlas from nearly two thousand years ago is a compelling example that bears comparison with modalities present in digital graphics today. Ingrid Hoelzl and Rémi Marie argue for thinking of images as "intrinsically merged with software" (2015, p. 7) in a sense that echoes the aesthetic, processual, and conceptual structuring of images through algorithms. They point out that the approach to mapmaking employed in Ptolemy's *Geography* (c. 150 CE) offers meaningful insight into the formulation of images in terms of algorithmic sets of instructions through a relatively simple, analog example in comparison to current forms directly involving the use of software. This chapter looks into what implications the geometric description of real-world phenomena in analog instructional practices may have for algorithmic media, drawing from diverse examples in addition to Ptolemy's *Geography*, including instructional approaches in anthropometric systems in drawing.

Contrary to what one might expect of an atlas, what can be found in the pages of Ptolemy's *Geography* is not a collection of images portraying the terrain and characteristics of various regions of the earth. Instead, the atlas is composed primarily of text: indexes listing locations and associated numbers, with a few diagrams illustrating how these are to be interpreted geometrically. *Geography* exists as more of a database than a visual depiction: a structured collection of written sets of coordinates, accompanied by instructions for how to read and draw maps from that data. Employing an analog methodology for storing and visually articulating spatial information, textually, *Geography* is notable for the way it reveals that algorithmic modalities may exceed the specificity of a given medium, technology, or time period. Hoelzl and Marie note that this has wide-ranging implications for the algorithmic tendencies in recent forms of image-making, namely departing from the paradigm of photography in a turn toward images being thought of as based on data.

As a program, the image, while still appearing as a geometrical projection on our screens, is inextricably mixed up with the data (physical and digital) and the continuous processing of these data.
(Hoelzl and Marie, 2015, p. 7)

In the sense that Hoelzl and Marie discuss, relationships between software and images have not been isolated to such instances directly involving the use of digital computers. As Miguel Carvalhais argues, computational aesthetics "hinges on the discovery of *what* a computational system does and *how* it operates" (2022, p. 39) in a way that allows us to see early aspects of the computational in media we might otherwise consider static. In this sense, aspects of Ptolemy's atlas, including the geometrical projection of spatial imagery from alphanumeric information, foreshadow methods and theories that have come to have central importance in recent discussions of algorithmic visual media.

One of Ptolemy's central innovations in *Geography* was the implementation of a coordinate system by which geographic locations may be plotted according to a grid. Demonstrating a method for geometrically modeling the world, this not only enabled proportional relationships to be maintained between geographic locations and features within a map, but it also permitted the transcription of images in textual form. An image may thus be created following written, algorithmic instructions or the reverse: starting from an image, one may transcribe written instructions for how to reproduce it. The Ptolemaic atlas thereby presents us with a rather elegant analog example of an algorithmic approach to image production, as well as touching upon the interrelation that may exist between images and texts.

Ptolemy's *Geography* places emphasis on the execution of images according to clearly defined, sequential operations. Providing written data and instructions for how to decode it into a visual depiction helped to solve the problem presented by the laborious task of duplicating maps by sight alone. Formulating the visual content of the atlas in a way that it could be transcribed in written form also made it easier to faithfully reproduce a map, as the reproductions would be based on the same coordinates. This held significance for the storage and transmission of spatial information, enabling the maps to be re-plotted even centuries after the atlas was originally composed. Transcoding an image or other artifact into an alphanumeric sequence facilitates its storage and transmission in the form of data, which is especially relevant to current contexts involving digital media.

The parameters defined by a given algorithmic system may afford degrees of variation, such as changes of scale while maintaining proportional measurements stable, granting images greater potential to be stored, printed, duplicated, or transmitted. Tying images to algorithmic procedure and to data — as opposed to a particular physical instantiation — renders them highly mutable, abundant, and transient. Algorithmic images may be understood as exceeding the singular execution as a physically individuated object. And, in some respects, they may also be integrative of the data and instructions these instantiations derive from. The possibility to have multiple readings of a given set of instructions endows algorithmic images with a mutability more commonly associated with computational media than with analog processes of image-making. For example, digital media can simulate other forms of media or to be read or expressed in more than one way across a variety of different media. The instructions for a given algorithmic image may be performed manually, but they also have a great deal of potentiality to be re-interpreted, misinterpreted, or iterated upon.

In a sense anticipating the seriality and iterability afforded to images by algorithmic approaches currently, *Geography* was not revolutionary for being an exclusively original work, but rather a reinterpretation from the work of another cartographer. *Geography* is primarily based on the maps and writings of Marinus of Tyre with only a few updates to select regions (Johnston, 1999). Consequently, Ptolemy's main contribution with this atlas was not the composition of the maps, themselves, but the methods he employed and explicated in its pages. The etymology of the word geography may be argued to echo this sentiment, by breaking the word down into the Greek "geo" and "graphein". In connecting the word to these origins, Johnston (1999) underlines the importance of the methodological approach employed, as well as the interrelationship between text and image. Following this logic, we can think of geography as a form of "earth writing" or "earth description", emphasizing geography not merely as a visualization of the world, in itself, but a way of visualizing the world.

Projections made using Ptolemy's methods resulted in maps that were aesthetically different from their predecessors, with the added functional implications that arose from creating maps that were more compatible with measurements of the territory represented. When the Ptolemaic atlas was translated from Greek to Latin in 1407, it conflicted with the then-current methods of medieval cartography, which at the time based the relative size of countries on power relations. As a result of Ptolemy's methods of mapmaking, the map becomes a closer reflection of real-world measurements than the mostly symbolic representations that were prevalent at the time. Beyond the aesthetic effect this had on the resulting maps, it also gave rise to a greater degree of accuracy in mapmaking. This is important not only for the relationship between maps and the world they are intended to represent but also for how they function as tools, affording particular kinds of relationships with that world. By changing the way that an image acts as a visual representation related to the world, a shift occurs in how that image, consequently, acts on it.

Hoelzl and Marie contend, in contrast to Ptolemy's own description of the atlas, that what he actually created with *Geography* was "not 'a representation in pictures of the whole known world' but a dataset that allowed Renaissance cartographers to draw what came to be known as the world's first accurate world maps" (p. 99). Rigorous attention to geometrical relationships and real-world data, as seen in the Ptolemaic maps, indicate a shift toward the development of a view of the world based on mathematic and scientific principles. In contrast to the more ideologically based and symbolic forms of representation that had been in place up to that point, the maps in *Geography* have not only internal geometric consistency between their compositional elements but these depictions are also intended to correspond to the relative size of objects in the real world.

In *Geography*, an analog algorithm acts as a structuring mechanism in the visual compositions of maps, allowing the internal proportional relationships between elements to be informed by geometric constraints. Hoelzl and Marie also point out that analog geometric compositional strategies were also employed in Ancient Egyptian and Roman art. Ancient Egyptian canons of representation involved systematic rules relevant to contemporary algorithmic media. In such cases, systematic constraints were used to standardize proportional relations internal to visual compositions. According to such an anthropometric system, the relative size of depicted figures and objects was made in accordance with pre-defined rules and units of measure that structured various motifs in relation to a grid.

Adherence to a geometric canon of representation allowed visual elements' height and width to be specified as multiples of units, enabling a degree of consistency to be maintained in the construction of visual compositions. For example, in Ancient Egyptian canonical representation, the proportions of a human figure would be defined as a set number of units in height and width, with each feature relative to those number of units. Constraining the execution of an image to a standard unit of measure, in this case, the cubit, allowed widespread unity in visual depictions. The cubit was a standard unit of measure in the Ancient world, since c. 3000 BCE. It was based on the length of the human forearm, measured from the elbow to the tip of the fingers. As it was based on a bodily measurement, the size of a cubit varied according to whose body was used as a reference. But as long as a depiction was produced according to the formula, its proportions would be the same as every other iteration.

Similar systematic use of geometric proportions to those employed in Ancient Egypt can be found in what is referred to as the *Vitruvian Man*. An anthropometric system of proportions, the *Vitruvian*

Man was outlined by the Roman architect Vitruvius in *De Architectura* c. 27 BCE. It is effectively a formula, according to which the male human body is drawn according to proportional relationships:

> **For the human body is so designed by nature that the face, from the chin to the top of the forehead and the lowest roots of the hair, is a tenth part of the whole height; the open hand from the wrist to the tip of the middle finger is just the same; the head from the chin to the crown is an eighth, and with the neck and shoulder from the top of the breast to the lowest roots of the hair is a sixth; from the middle of the breast to the summit of the crown is a fourth.**
> **(Vitruvius, c. 27 BCE., p. 72)**

Following such an algorithmic description, the depiction of the human body is thereby guided by formulaic instructions, which constrain its dimensions. While such image-making methods may employ mathematical constraints on the proportions of the depiction of human bodies, they are more concerned with notions of compositional harmony than with representational precision in the sense of producing realistic or accurate depictions. Though based to some extent on direct measurements of actual human bodies, they are generalized, using average sizes of bodily features to approximate a norm from multiple bodies. In addition to working from direct measurements of human bodily proportions, Vitruvius's anthropometric system also sought to invoke what were thought of as divine relationships in geometry:

> **If a man be placed flat on his back, with his hands and feet extended, and a pair of compasses centred at his navel, the fingers and toes of his two hands and feet will touch the circumference of a circle described therefrom. And just as the human body yields a circular outline, so too a square figure may be found from it. For if we measure the distance from the soles of the feet to the top of the head, and then apply that measure to the outstretched arms, the breadth will be found to be the same as the height, as in the case of plane surfaces which are perfectly square.**
> **(Vitruvius, c. 27 BCE., p. 73)**

Circles, squares, the Fibonacci sequence, and the golden ratio were seen as having special properties and they held connotations of perfection, balance, symmetry, and unity. Using these as guiding principles of visual aesthetics, such as in the *Vitruvian Man*, sought to draw on conceptual associations through their structuring of spatial relationships. The best-known example of the *Vitruvian Man* is that drawn by Leonardo da Vinci, where the body of a man is aligned within the proportions of a square and circle.

Echoes of these ancient compositional strategies can also be found in modernist design and architecture. For example, Le Corbusier's *Modulor* man (1945), was intended as a design tool that would facilitate particular aesthetic relations in design and architecture, relative to the proportions of the human body. Aimed at achieving a degree of aesthetic unity, Le Corbusier defined a systematic approach to the relative measurements of designed objects and spaces. Of the *Modulor* system, he said:

> **Various measures are now in use:**
> **The inch and foot by the British (it kept their architecture related to human proportions in spite of the machine age). The meter, derived**

from the meridian of the globe, is an artificial and arbitrary measure that has nothing to do with human proportions and which, as a result, has led to a certain disintegration in the architecture of those countries which used it. In view of the immense task of manufacture and prefabrication to be completed, a unified scale of measurement based on the human body had to be created, a highly significant mathematical expression capable of giving innumerable combinations that are really satisfactory and above all harmonious.
(Le Corbusier)

Le Corbusier's development of the *Modulor* man with the intention of informing the design of functional objects and spaces shows how the same principles used in two-dimensional visual compositions and images may also be applied to three-dimensional contexts such as in architecture. This dimensional application of geometric proportions draws an interesting parallel with the cubit, which was employed both in visual compositions on flat surfaces and built constructions. Its specific emphasis on geometrical harmony also recalls the same quality in Vitruvius's system.

Bringing the structuring principles of algorithmic compositional strategies into the design of functional objects and spaces adds a dimension of interactivity that is relevant to our later discussion of how algorithmic forms of visual media may be understood as not just shaping visual aesthetics, but also acting on the world. It's noteworthy that in the *Vitruvian Man,* the human figure is normalized as an European adult male, which is described in terms of its presumed universality. The *Modulor* man is even more specific, tailored to the bodily proportions of an idealized average French man. Positioning such a particular demographic as if it is neutral raises similar issues to those that arise in the tendency of machine learning systems to reiterate and even amplify existing patterns and biases. This is illustrative of how specific assumptions and value judgments may be embedded in an algorithmic system before it is even employed. Recalling Hoelzl and Marie's description of algorithmic methodologies as not producing visualizations, but acting as a mode of visualization, Luciana Parisi argues in her book *Contagious Architecture* (2013, p. 102–7) that *parametricism* imposes a particular logic upon not only on design but also on interaction with its constructions. According to this perspective, algorithms may be understood to inform not only the outputs of the processes in which they are applied but also the relationships such designed objects and structures have with the world around them.

In each of the cases discussed in this chapter, a set of proportional rules establishes particular mathematical relationships between compositional elements and the human body. These strategies inform the production of images, both in terms of the processes involved, but also guiding the geometric relationships within compositions. In this sense, anthropometric systems such as Ancient Egyptian canonical representation, the *Vitruvian Man* and the *Modulor* system demonstrate how algorithmic relationships can be used to inform visual media, processually, and aesthetically. They also invite comparison with strategies that are currently employed in art and design contexts through comparatively simple methods. It is possible to produce images according to the analog methods described here manually, using only simple tools, whereas more complex, automated image-making systems can be relatively opaque to human understanding.

Looking at analog instances in which systematic implementation of mathematical relationships and algorithmic sets of instructions are used to determine visual outputs enables us to recognize similar compositional strategies across vastly different applications and time periods. Establishing median values for the representation of a human figure based on multiple real-world measurements, as we saw in the *Vitruvian Man,* bears resemblance to the development of statistical models in machine learning, which are based on the analysis of numerous examples. In parametric design and architecture, complex mathematical relationships inform the design of objects and urban spaces. This draws a parallel with *approximation,* which in mathematics describes the use of a simpler function in place of another to achieve a more accurate result specific to a given context. Describing real-world phenomena mathematically through the development of models facilitates understanding them in new ways, a theme that cuts across these fairly diverse examples.

Hoelzl and Marie (2015) argue that *Geography* demonstrates a turn towards "the world as database" in which "software [...] is also part of the structure of the image" (p. 83) As they describe, images, now, are often taken as visual representations of the world based on data. According to this perspective, data-based images are not merely visual depictions of the world, but rather, visual depictions derived from data about the world, representing:

> **A world that does not exist in and for itself, but only insofar as its natural and cultural resources and its inhabitants are transformed into the common language of symbols and numbers that allow their universal commensurability.**
> **(Hoelzl and Marie, 2015, p. 100)**

This is a significant philosophical distinction that lies at the heart of how technologically mediated imaging — including, but not exclusive to algorithmic media — may meaningfully depart from or connect to other image paradigms. While the idea of images *as* or *based* on data is one we are quite familiar with today, it is important to recognize that it has not always been a pervasive view of visual media. It is a construct that has been built up over time with quite specific built-in value judgments, cutting across diverse media and time periods. Treating images as interchangeable with, representative of, or the product of data affords certain technical modalities, such as those explored in this chapter or more complex processes covered later in this book, but it also imposes a particular logic on the outcomes of such processes.

As we will further examine in later chapters, the idea of the image as a database offers a useful perspective on images created using machine learning, which have a relatively direct relationship to visual data in comparison to other forms of image-making. This may be thought of in several ways, for example, that training a machine learning model requires many images that ultimately inform the production of generated images. We may also think of machine learning-generated images as a form of data, although this comes with the caveat that machine learning has a demonstrated tendency towards bias and error that undermines the presumptions of objectivity typically associated with data-based processes.

The following chapter expands on the idea that the transcription of images in terms of data or algorithmic sets of instructions, as in the examples covered here, affords images particular qualities that extend beyond attempts at merely capturing or replicating visual appearances. This leads us to discuss the implications of transcodability, seriality, latency, and iterability in image-making, which are important to our later consideration of generative strategies and highly automated forms of visual media. These aspects tie into discussions in later chapters of this book concerning instruction-based practices and the operative image.

TRANSCRIPTION

By allowing visual compositions to be formulated according to pre-defined instructions, procedures, and constraints, algorithmic approaches to image production emphasize images' *transmedial* capacity to "unfold across multiple media platforms, with each medium making distinctive contributions to our understanding of the world" (Jenkins, 2006, p. 293). For example, we may think of a digital image file on a hard drive, in terms relative to the same image file when it is displayed on a screen or printed on paper. And while a given media artifact is thus understood as exceeding beyond the specificity of any particular medium, the qualities of the medium where a given instantiation plays out can be seen to inform its qualities. Transcribing instructions for the production of images in written form highlights their capacity to be stored, transmitted, and transcoded between various formats. It also gives the production of images a level of continuity across these instantiations. Repeating the same procedure, for example, enables a given image to be replicated — in theory — endlessly, in a variety of different iterations, between which the image can be understood as existing in latent, unarticulated form.

In addition to contributing to the reproducibility of images, and the automation of that process, algorithmic formulations also give rise to nuanced interrelationships between texts and images, which contributes to the view of images as a form of data or as interchangeable with it. These aspects impact how we think about the ontological status of images, due to the fact that they enable an image to be understood as exceeding beyond a singular, fixed, and materially individuated object. In this way, the transmediality of images raises similar issues to the difficulties encountered in attempts at defining art, especially in response to conceptual artists' experimental, instruction-based methodologies to artistic production placed emphasis on concepts and processes over the material and visual qualities of art objects. Considering these qualities of algorithmic image production through ideas explored in conceptualism, this chapter looks at how the use of instruction-based methods has contributed to theoretical perspectives on images and art.

Rather than materially fixed and stable objects, algorithmic artifacts like images and art emphasize process and tend towards a lack of media specificity. Given that the same algorithm can be performed in a variety of different ways using a diversity of different media, the outcomes can likewise be diverse. In this sense, the transmediality of images renders them ontologically difficult to pin down, as it endows a given image with a dramatic variability in terms of its potential instantiations, for example, that may exist in forms that are material or immaterial, visual or non-visual, constructed by hand or by highly automated machines. For example, in the case of systems that generate images based on text prompts, the relationship between text and image feels quite direct, enabling images and words to be treated as interchangeable. Natural language thereby acts as an interface through which to develop a representation within a machine learning system and to output the results of such an analytical process in the form of a digital image.

Though more often associated with digital media, transmedial qualities can also be found in pre-digital examples of algorithmic visual media. By enabling images to be more easily transmitted in the form of alphanumeric code, for example, transcoding endows them with greater degrees of latency. As we recall from our earlier discussion of *Geography* (Ptolemy, c. 150 CE) that the transcodability of images formulated in terms of a written codex made it possible to replot Ptolemy's maps thousands of years after their original formulation. This quality also allows us to recognize a level of continuity between the image and the instructions for its execution. Though these are not directly interchangeable, the image, as such, may be understood as conveyed in a variety of forms, including textual or pictorial.

The transcription of spatial data in textual form enables images to be written down as a collection of coordinates with instructions for how this data could be interpreted into a visual representation. The temporal lag between capturing, creating, or writing an image and reading, visualizing, or experiencing it may be, in theory, indefinite. In the case of *Geography*, this aspect of latency is taken to an extreme, with a span of hundreds or even thousands of years between the transcription of instructions and the eventual execution of the maps in visual form. This example demonstrates how the transcodability of images in the form of algorithmic instructions for their later execution affords them the potential to exist in a latent state, suspended between capture and articulation.

In the temporal delay between formulating an image algorithmically and its expression in visual form, the latent image is not perceptually accessible to human viewers, nor is it materially instantiated in a form that is intelligible as a distinct entity. For example, we may understand a degree of unity between copies of a given image file, a sort of singular plurality (Nancy, 2000). Not solely singular, while at the same time being multiples of a one, such an instance enables us to think beyond conceptions of images and art objects, for that matter, as unique, one-of-a-kind entities. More than merely a virtual image that has the potential to come into existence, the latent image has durational qualities that are significant to our understanding of the increasingly processual aspects of visual media. Between the trigger of the shutter release and the production of an analog photograph, the latent image takes on several different forms. The play of light off of objects onto film is in turn used to direct the exposure of photosensitive paper that is then developed and finally fixed.

Digital media's instantaneity may easily obscure any delay in image processing relative to that of developing an analog photograph. Nevertheless, even if it may be so short as to be rendered virtually imperceptible, the temporality of creating an image using a digital camera draws attention to the physicality actually entailed in such processes. In digital photography, *latency* refers to the time it takes for photons to be processed from the camera's sensor into the digital image that is then displayed. Sean Cubitt, Daniel Palmer, and Nathaniel Tkacz (2015) explain:

> **Both digital and analog imaging require periods of latency, the one awaiting chemical amplification in the developing process, the other the draining of electrons from the chip prior to the next exposure, a feature that makes clear that there is no difference to be sought in the constant visibility of analog as opposed to digital images.**
> **(Cubitt, Palmer and Tkacz, 2015, p. 16)**

Considering the interpretation of light into stored data that occurs through the sensor of the digital camera offers insight into the materiality of digital images. It helps us to think about the transmediality of digital images, as although they may defy medium specificity and can be articulated, stored, or transmitted across various material forms, it would be inaccurate to say that they are entirely immaterial. Digital artifacts may confound existing ideas of an image as singular, materially fixed, two-dimensional, and finite. W. J. T. Mitchell (1986) notes that "the image never appears except in some medium or another, but it is also what transcends media, what can be transferred from one medium to another" (p. 16).

By allowing a given image to be performed repeatedly following the same instructions or composing those instructions in terms such that the same task may be performed by programmed machines, the formulation of images in terms of defined constraints and procedures facilitates seriality and automation in ways that have been historically significant in assessments of cultural artifacts. This is informed by Walter Benjamin's (1935) assessments of the effects that mechanical automation had on the products of industrialized, serial production, which we will discuss at greater length later in the chapter *Automation*. Addressing related aspects specific to digital and networked content, Alexander Galloway (2011) captures the peculiar materiality of data-based images, saying: "Consider the case of Wikipedia, a singular (data) image produced by thousands and thousands of end-users on their laptops" (p. 94). This understanding of the dispersed materiality of images resonates with Timothy Morton's (2013) conception of *hyperobjects,* described as "massively distributed in time and space relative to humans" (p. 1). Thinking of images in such terms enables us to consider their paradoxical omnipresence and dispersion. The image as a hyperobject would include the multitudes of materially-articulated images and visual data that exist, which are not physically situated in discrete locations and times, but rather have ethereal properties that coexist with temporal endurance.

In addition to their potential for ephemerality and iterability, the spatial qualities of images arguably add to the theoretical trouble in narrowing in on the material characteristics of images. As we recall from our discussion of parametric design and architecture, the same qualities applied in simple, geometric systems of proportion can also be applied in the enactment of multi-dimensional objects and spaces. The capacity for a given digital object to exist in a spatialized form is explored in Artnode's *File Room* (2017). The work centered on materializing a selection of digital artifacts from the art group's collection of web-based files, which the artist group presented in the form of 3D-printed sculptures produced by reinterpreting various file formats into 3D objects. Thinking of such examples as image objects, as Jacob Gaboury (2021) proposes, we can consider these kinds of digital/material entities as "neither images nor objects" that "exist in a lenticular state that shifts with our perception of them" (p. 202). In the materialized digital files created by Artnode or other cases in which a digital entity is physically manifested in various ways, it is notable that the capacity of digital image files to be instantiated, in theory, in any format problematizes the limits of what an image is. If images may take on any form, material, immaterial, or informational, visual or non-visual, then *what is not an image*? (Parikka, 2023, p. 57) This raises the question of where the boundaries may lie between image and non-image. It's not a great stretch of the imagination to think about 3D graphics as objects or 3D-printed objects as images. But it may then water down the definition to the point of being untenable.

The material variability of images makes it difficult to outline what qualities constitute an image, since in theory, an image may take on a diverse range of attributes. Defining what an image is thus remains an enduring problem in image studies that is notably explored by Mitchell in his well-known text *What is an*

Image? (1986). While the development of image ontologies continues to pose theoretical challenges more than thirty years after Mitchell's examination of the issue, some fruitful discussions have come from exploring what qualities of images render them so philosophically problematic. Relevant discussions have recently picked up this thread, emphasizing how the effects of recent technological developments are reflected in what has been referred to as the "changing ontology of the Image" (Lund, 2021).

Resolving the issue of what an image is — or is not — is too complex an issue to resolve here, and it remains an open problem within the field of image studies. But what matters for our purposes is that an image may exceed its instantiation in any specific medium, technology, or method employed in its articulation. Algorithms did not single-handedly endow images with the capacity to transcend beyond a single instantiation or medium but rather contribute to new forms and new forms of visibility for this phenomenon. As we recall from discussing the parallel forms of latency in analog and digital photography, aspects such as transcodability or latency may exist in different ways in "new media" than their predecessors without a fundamental change of paradigm taking place.

Without answering his own question concerning what an image is outright, Mitchell (1986) explores the variable ways of being available to images in his "family tree of images" (p. 9). According to this perspective, a given image may be articulated across a variety of different media, maintaining levels of consistency between, for example, mental-, textual-, and visual images. To illustrate, Mitchell includes textual, sonic, verbal, and mental images in this breakdown, arguing that an image may exist in such forms while maintaining its ontological status as an image. Farocki (2004) examined similar interrelationships between objects and their enaction through various forms of media, and he traced his own use of the term "operative image" (p. 17) back to Roland Barthes' (1957) distinction between objective language and meta-language (p. 146). In the passage quoted by Farocki in *Phantom Images,* Barthes discusses language as "operative" in the sense that it has the capacity to act — or operate — upon the world:

> **I "speak the tree," I do not speak about it. This means that my language is operational, transitively linked to its object; between the tree and myself, there is nothing but my la-**

bour, that is to say, an action. This is a political language: it represents nature for me only inasmuch as I am going to transform it, it is a language thanks to which I "act the object;" the tree is not an image for me, it is simply the meaning of my action.
(Barthes, 1957, p. 146)

This sense of the transformative operation of language on objects in the world is helpful when we think about the enaction, temporality, and meaning of images. It not only allows us to emphasize relationships between language and the production of images, that they may be formulated verbally or textually, but this also foreshadows perspectives that focus specifically on the processual qualities entailed therein.

Art has undergone similar transmutations to those of the image, both of which bear the effects and after-effects of the many technical processes that have become embedded in everyday life and, consequently, culture. The transmediality of images is paralleled in what Lucy Lippard (1973) referred to as the *dematerialization of the art object* in mid-20th-century art. Rather than abolishing the materiality of art objects outright, this concept described shifting perspectives on the materiality and aesthetics of art objects, which came to be seen as secondary to other qualities, namely, their intellectual impact. Conceptually-engaged artists explored the capacity for artworks and ideas to be thought of as transmedial and exceeding beyond a single, material instantiation, which led to new conceptions of not only what art could be, but also what criteria were to be employed in judging it.

The idea that an image or artwork may exist in latent form or be actualized according to sets of instructions has been influential in the work of conceptual artists, such as Sol LeWitt. Especially well known for his wall drawings that emphasize the use of instructions and that may be instantiated in more than one way, many of LeWitt's works involve the implementation of proportional relationships that are relative to the context where they are installed. This renders the drawings to some extent variable, each instance being unique to the given parameters, in spite of being based on the same set of instructions. Dividing a wall into a given number of sections, within which lines are drawn at specific angles or using various colors, the instructions for a work allow a given work of art to be formalized in terms of specific constraints that exceed their material instantiation as a physically actualized artwork, as such.

As LeWitt (1969) wrote in his *Sentences on Conceptual Art*, "for each work of art that becomes physical there are many variations that do not", suggesting that the artistic potentiality of a work exceeds that which becomes actualized, materially. A similar perspective on the conceptual and material basis of instructional approaches to art is articulated by Lawrence Weiner (1968) in his *Declaration of Intent* where he says:

> **1. The artist may construct the piece.**
> **2. The piece may be fabricated.**
> **3. The piece need not be built.**
> **Each being equal and consistent with the intent of the artist the decision as to condition rests with the receiver upon the occasion of receivership.**

Following this logic, like images, concepts, too, may be physically manifested in various ways, including the possibility for non-instantiation. Weiner's statement that "the piece need not be built" allows us to understand the art object as independent from its actualization as a finished object. With these statements, Weiner opens the possibility for alternative perspectives to traditional framings concerning the creation of artworks. Firstly, by asserting that an artist's construction may be seen as incidental, rather than crucial to an artwork's existence, he takes the emphasis off conceptions of artistic authorship as a determining factor in the potential for something to be viewed as an artwork. He thereby allows for the non-execution of a piece, meaning that its ontological status does not hinge on its actualization in perceivable form. By explicitly invoking the audience as the "receiver" of a work of art, Weiner also places a degree of intentionality and responsibility on the act of experiencing the piece. In this sense, one is not passively subjected to the work of art but rather participates in its reception.

Similar issues to those raised by Weiner and LeWitt concerning the possibility for someone other than the artist to construct a work of art also come up in connection with Marcel Duchamp's final artwork, *Étant donnés,* which he worked on from 1946 until his death in 1968. Prior to that date, the work had already been acquired and was intended as a gift to the Philadelphia Museum of Art, but due to the artist's unexpected demise, he never touched the final instantiation of the work, itself. Preparators at the Philadelphia Museum of Art used a manual of instructions Duchamp had compiled, containing meticulous notes and photographs detailing how *Étant donnés* should be dismantled and reinstalled in the museum.

> **In his title page for the manual, Duchamp refers to Étant donnés... as an "approximation démontable" (an approximation that can be taken apart, or disassembled), adding that in using the word "approximation" he intends to convey a margin of ad libitum in the assembly and disassembly of his construction.**
> **(Philadelphia Museum of Art, 2009)**

Recalling the theme of the previous chapter of this book, this description of the work as an approximation and iterable seems to allude to the idea that a work's essence may exceed its individual instantiation, with the possibility of existing in more than one configuration. Beyond these aspects related to its reconstruction based on instructions outlined in a manual, *Étant donnés* also entails a highly specific framing of the viewer's gaze that can be thought of as relevant to the algorithmic structuring of visual compositions. The piece requires viewers to peer through a set of peepholes to see a dimensional assemblage reminiscent of a diorama. In this way, the sculptural work is visually flattened into something akin to a spatial image, whose depth is compressed by the constrained point of view.

A related example that zeroes in on the performative act of a viewer's reception of a work of art is Yoko Ono's *Instruction Paintings*, which are collected in the book *Grapefruit* (1964). With an explicit emphasis on highly perceptual language, the "paintings" are exhibited in textual form and intended to be articulated conceptually by the audience. Describing these written instructions as paintings and often directing viewers to imagine experiential qualities and situations, Ono conjures what Mitchell (1986) would call "mental images" (p. 9) that are manifested through thinking. For instance, by directing the audience to construct paintings, either in their own head or physically, through various actions, the artist gives them an aesthetic experience that is on the one hand connected to the art object, while disconnected from its specificity. The instantiation of the artwork takes shape through its material actualization in the form of written instructions that are exhibited, the conceptual experience of the work articulated in the minds of those that experience it, and it could extend to the performance of the actions described.

By arguing for the immateriality of the work of art, explorations with instruction-based approaches by conceptual artists develop notions of immaterial artifacts that may or may not be constructed, physically, without being explicitly bound to their material instantiation, per se. This also served as a way of considering language or the instructions for the production of systematic works as a conceptual tool for art. The physical artwork may be seen, on the one hand, as superfluous to the concept of the work, in which case the instructions take precedence over its material manifestation. Or it can be argued that through viewing the product of instructional procedures, those instructions and structured processes are engaged by viewers. In such cases, formal procedures, ideas, and interpretive processes may be more important to the experience and understanding of a work than its specific visual or material qualities.

Although this chapter gets us no closer to resolving the problem of understanding what an image is, it seeks to enrich our perspective on why that is the case through similar issues in defining art. Algorithmic approaches to image-making add to existing difficulty in defining what an image is and is not. Endowing the creation of images with dramatic variability, algorithmic formulations of images allow multiples of the same image to be made according to the same instructions, and for these to be materially and visually instantiated in diverse ways across media. This also affords the possibility for images to exist in a latent state that is inaccessible to human visual perception, a paradox that goes against the grain of traditional conceptions of images primarily in visual terms. In these ways, the transmediality of images raises theoretical difficulties in the development of image ontologies. As in the dematerialization of the art object, images may defy attempts at defining them in strictly visual or material terms.

Through the dematerialization of the art object, or rather, shifting perspectives on its ontological status, we can also follow a parallel shift in thinking about the material conditions entailed in the production of images. This aspect is especially visible in digital and networked images, which can be reproduced and even iterated upon at will. In addition to affording the proliferation of endless amounts of copies of a given image, formulating images in terms of clearly defined sets of algorithmic instructions highlights images' capacity to be articulated variously across a range of media. Thinking of the unarticulated image in terms of latency, we see that algorithmic formulations facilitate particular interrelationships between images and texts, instructions, and data. Images' potential transmission in the form of data also renders them closer to information than seeing them as solely objects that are defined by their visual qualities.

AUTOMATION

Formulating the production of images algorithmically lays the foundations for visual tasks to be carried out by machines, enabling the production of images to be performed repeatedly, uniformly, and often more quickly, with less investment of human effort than entailed in manual methods. Seriality, acceleration, and the displacement of human labor became hallmarks of industrialization, calling into question traditional criteria for the assessment of cultural value, such as uniqueness, handicraft, and material worth. Automation therefore triggered a cultural reckoning with its effects on both the process of creating a given object, the object itself, and the role of authorship. It continues to be a significant factor in discourse on cultural artifacts, especially regarding the increasing influence and arguably creative role of machine learning in the production of digital content. Although it has often been viewed negatively by cultural critics, more nuanced views on automation have emerged, adapting to the changing conditions afforded by technical developments in visual media.

Automation is a recurring theme in the evaluation of images, especially concerning the value of human labor it may displace. Although they involve different processes, related arguments to this have been applied to a wide range of visual technologies, from the widespread use of mechanized printing and analog photographic processes to recent forms of digital imaging that entail so little direct human intervention that they may be thought of as *nonhuman photography* (Zylinska, 2017). Due to the increasing ubiquity, processing power, and autonomy of machines in visual media, automation remains a significant factor in how we think about the production of images in terms of the level of intentionality expressed by humans or machines. Examining this through historical tendencies in discourse about the conceptual value associated with the objects of automated processes, this chapter considers the position of human perception and agency in relation to visual technologies.

In *The Work of Art in the Age of Mechanical Reproduction,* Walter Benjamin (1935) famously argued that mechanical reproducibility threw traditional criteria for the evaluation of art into contention. Central to this argument is the idea that by enabling a given object — or image, for that matter — be, in theory, reproduced endlessly, mechanized production processes may undermine the conceptual value imbued in objects. Technological reproducibility, he argued, resulted in a loss, decay, or withering of the aura imparted in objects through human labor:

> **It might be stated as a general formula that the technology of reproduction detaches the reproduced object from the sphere of tradition. By replicating the work many times over, it substitutes a mass existence for a unique existence. And in permitting the reproduction to reach the recipient in his or her own situation, it actualizes that which is reproduced. (p. 22)**

Prior to the Industrial era, beyond their cultural importance, the worth of images, art objects, or other artifacts could at least to some extent be measured in terms of invested hours of — human — labor. But this kind of metric was upended by technologies that displaced human labor, as well as making industrialized products more easily replicable and therefore faster and cheaper to produce. If a product can be created using a machine to reduce the required investment of time, effort, and skilled labor to one made by hand, for example, and the results are materially indistinguishable from one another, how are we to understand the relationship between the two? Comparisons between manually produced objects to those produced using automated machines resulted in the process of making something being considered a factor in qualitative judgments of such products, as well as art and visual artifacts such as images.

How a work of art was produced thereby came to be seen as relevant contextual information for looking at its aesthetic qualities. The idea of art as a process is now quite familiar, but this is a fairly recent development in the history of art. Rather than fixating solely on the inherent qualities of art objects, in themselves, art in the early 20th century began to consider other factors that inform art including the processes involved in its production. Experimentation with instructional approaches, especially in conceptual art, has allowed images — and art objects, for that matter — to be seen as exceeding their material instantiation as physically individuated objects. This has contributed to a view inclusive of contextual factors and external information as relevant to understanding the significance of cultural artifacts.

These ideas were radically challenged in contemporary art over the course of the 20th century. Especially notable explorations on this topic include the concept of the readymade proposed by Marcel Duchamp or Andy Warhol's preoccupation with mass media as well as mass-production techniques and aesthetics. Asked in an interview about his choice to use a mass-produced object to create a work of art, Duchamp expressed a degree of ambivalence about the intention to create a work of art and remarked that he felt that the term readymade "thrust itself upon" him, explaining: "It seemed perfect for these things that weren't works of art, that weren't sketches, and to which no art terms applied" (Cabanne, 1967, p. 47–48). Arguing for the artistic value of appropriation emphasized the artist's role in curating, presenting, and contextualizing something, over the direct creation of an object or that object's aesthetic qualities and considerations of taste. Presenting industrially produced objects as works of art, artists invoked audiences to question whether a mass-produced object may be considered valuable, and to what degree its inherent characteristics, creation, or context play a role in how we evaluate objects.

Explorations such as those led by artists such as Duchamp led to transformative discussions in contemporary art's reckonings with automation, they did not manage to resolve the issue outright. While nascent technocultural paradigms subsequent to those discussed by Benjamin in 1935 have entailed different particularities, ongoing discourse has often echoed a similar focus on the shifting role of human labor as a result of technical developments in production processes. While this may appear to represent a distinct polarity, in which either the human or the machine is exclusively responsible for a given outcome, there is more interplay between these perspectives than meets the eye. Backtracking to much earlier examples of automated processes in visual media, we examine how discussions around this theme draw on contrasting expressions of human agency, authorship, and artistry with the increasingly automated performance of visual tasks by machines.

The mechanization of print media is acknowledged as a significant step in the tendency toward automated, serialized production of visual media. Seriality had long been achievable using techniques such as the woodcut or lithograph, to produce multiple images from a single plate, but mechanization allowed multiples of a given text, image, or text-image to be produced more quickly, easily, and, consequently, often with less investment of resources. The invention of moveable type is attributed in Western contexts to Johannes Gutenberg, who created a movable-type printing press in c. 1440 that bears his name and is credited for introducing and popularizing letterpress printing in Europe. The Gutenberg press greatly accelerated the rate at which books could be printed, which consequently made them more affordable and widespread. This contributed to a dramatic shift in the communication of information and knowledge, which Marshall McLuhan (1962) referred to as the "Gutenberg Revolution". In this case, automation is understood as enmeshed with a number of factors that led to changing perspectives on the value of cultural productions.

The development of analog photography gave rise to a similar reckoning with the implications of automation for evaluations of visual media. Photography is now widely accepted as an artistic medium but was in its early years argued to be inferior to painting on the grounds that automation took the skill or creative expression of the human. At the time photography began to become widespread, a considerable amount of time, labor, and skill would have been required in order to manually produce an image comparable to a photograph. Prior to analog photography, earlier forms of optical media such as the camera obscura had enabled highly realistic projections to be made, but the possibility to fix an optically-derived image, as in analog photographic processes, shifted optical media from an event — often part public spectacle, part scientific demonstration — to a fixed object.

Printed photographs drew comparison with other forms, such as paintings, although their potential as art was fiercely debated. Interestingly, similar arguments to those aimed at delegitimizing photography as an artistic medium have been made to legitimize its scientific objectivity. One aspect of this argument is that by distancing the process of image-making from the subjectivity and intentionality of a human author, the technical apparatus imbues the image with a greater degree of truthfulness. This framing of photography also relies on the idea of the directness of capturing an image of an object or view.

In addition to allowing images to be produced and replicated, formulating images in terms of pre-defined sets of instructions also facilitates the potential the creation of new content. Procedurally-driven practices (Carvalhais, 2016) and conceptual strategies for content generation were pioneered by artists long before digital computers were accessible or widespread, emphasizing the enactment of processes and the function of systems. Many times, this involves forfeiting degrees of control, allowing the process to produce unpredictable results within particular constraints, using recombination, chance, and randomization to achieve emergent results. Such strategies for approaching the timeless problem of staring at a blank page bring up modalities familiar in current computational methods, though they are now often framed in terms of artificial intelligence.

The idea of giving over agency or intentionality to a process or machine gained traction at the beginning of the 20th century in Surrealist *automatism*. Dada and Surrealist artists often used sets of instructions as a sort of artistic program to be interpreted or orchestrated, combining systems of rules with elements of randomness or unpredictability. This kind of approach experiments with the concept of automatism, entailing deliberate engagement with factors beyond the artist's control. Similar ideas also arise in Surrealist *automatism*, which emerged from automatic writing and drawing. These practices were varied and had diverse intentions and idea systems behind them, such as seeking to engage with either spirits or the individual's subconscious, channeling these apparent influences into texts and images, and later, art objects. But at its core, the idea of automatism was to dissociate oneself from conscious control over the creative process, allowing other aspects to express themselves in what is thus produced. Some of the basic techniques and ideas behind automatism in art continue to occupy theorists today, especially the use of unpredictable processes and relationships between human and nonhuman agency.

Recombination (Carvalhais, 2016, p. 146), the rearrangement of components within a system, is an important modality of many algorithmically-engaged artistic practices. A famous example of this is the cut-up method used by Dada artists in the 1920s and later by Brion Gysin and William S. Burroughs in the 1950s and into the 1970s. The cut-up technique can be — and has been — applied to a variety of different media, but its defining aspect involves partitioning an initial object and rearranging those parts into a new formation. The end result of such a process can merely be a stage in the progression of producing a work, or it can be seen as a finished work in itself. Exposing some of the ambiguity between a work in itself and a work as an ongoing process, Situationist maps such as those produced by Guy Debord were often constructed from cutting up and recomposing fragments of maps in effort to break from habitual patterns of behavior. They are not intended to be viewed, strictly, as objects in themselves, but rather as scripts or scores to be interpreted and acted out by viewers. Following such a map results in a practice called the *dérive*, or drift, a technique of redirecting one's attention and movement in ways that dissociate from customary routine navigation in favor of new, experimental, and serendipitous experiences of one's urban surroundings.

Mimicking aspects of the machinic, the idea of automatism, as well as Dadaist and Surrealist recourse to randomness, absurdity, and meaninglessness seem especially fitting as a reaction to the increasingly structured nature of modern, urban, industrial life, and to the senselessness of world events at that time they were working. Within the context of the interwar period, as well as coinciding with widespread automation and the rise of mass media, Dada and Surrealist artists addressed major shifts that were occurring, socially, as well as materially. Not only was there a great reckoning with the aftermath of World War I, with the destruction and lack of control it entailed, but industrialization was also altering manufacturing, and with it, attitudes towards work and the value of the products of that labor. In response to this context, artists experimenting with automatism explored ways of delegating artistic decision-making to processes, machines, or collaboration with other people.

Engaging with experiments with what was an unconventional stance towards meaning in art at the beginning of the twentieth century. Playing with the idea that some parts of art and/or artistic production are not inherently meaningful and could be delegated to a random process or even automated using a machine goes against certain artistic dogmas surrounding art and the act of artistic creation. These ideas have by now been mostly normalized within contemporary art, although they resurface in certain respects, especially in relation to the use of new and emerging technologies in art. The use of instructions in art has also been important in the development of generative art, in which artists have explored the use of autonomous systems that in turn create emergent behavior.

The randomness and unpredictability of recombinant strategies afford the exploration of existing material and structures in new ways. These modalities can also be used to not only recombine fragments but to generate new content. A common approach to the incorporation of unpredictability is the use of chance-based procedures such as the roll of a die. In digital media, this may take the form of pseudorandom numbers generated by computers. Procedural strategies may be used in an explorative capacity, methodically directing or structuring experimentation within a particular realm of possibilities, or search space. Such explorative approaches are often found in generative approaches that employ variation within a set of pre-defined constraints. In such cases, the creative potential of algorithms to produce surprising results may be implemented to produce new visual content or as a driving conceptual force in a work.

Generative approaches often seek to allow something other than the direct human decision-making of the artist to play a role in directing the outcome. The aim of using such methods is usually to engage levels of variation within defined constraints, enabling artists to draw influence from, complement, or redirect the progression of a work. But while generative approaches are, at least in theory, open to potentially endless variation, it's important to note the limitations that this has on generative artworks. In generative approaches to machine learning, algorithms may produce surprising results that are difficult to predict. This is relevant not only to how the processes employed influence the characteristics of their outputs but also to how the role of such processes is viewed, for instance, that algorithms and algorithmic processes may act in complement to the intentionality of the human author.

This offers an interesting parallel to the use of similar approaches to the incorporation of computational processes in art, which despite differing tools, media, and aesthetics, shares a similar preoccupation with process. In assessing the outcomes of generative approaches in art, similar issues arise to those brought up in relation to much earlier methods. For example, variation for its own sake lends itself to quite different results from variation that is applied in an explorative capacity. Strategies involving chance and unpredictability may indeed produce new, different results each time they are performed, but without meaningful constraints or direction, they are unlikely to produce results that are interesting.

Perspectives have shifted over the course of the 20th and early 21st century to not only accommodate but even exalt seriality, ephemerality, strategies of appropriation, and the use of technology in contemporary art. Nevertheless, the idea of machine participation in art or even authorship of it has proven to be an enduring theme in discourse across several fields including art history and criticism, and media studies, and it remains a popular way of framing projects that bridge art and engineering.

Similar ideas were raised in early explorations on the topics of cybernetics, robotics, and art. Jasia Reichardt — curator of the groundbreaking exhibition *Cybernetic Serendipity* presented at the Institute of Contemporary Arts, London, in 1968 — recalls a poignant anecdote on the topic of machine- or AI- authorship from her experience working with the artist Harold Cohen. Best known for his work developing an artificial intelligence system that he named AARON in his artistic practice since the 1960s, Cohen reached a point of being unsure of whether to consider himself or his system as being the author of the artworks it produced. In response to this ambiguity, according to Reichardt, Cohen went so far as coloring on top of AARON's drawings in an apparent effort to prevent his importance from being eclipsed by that of the machine he had designed. Cohen's internal struggle for authorship is also evident in his alternation between signing images with his own signature, AARON's signature, or a combination of both, as described by Reichardt in her 2018 talk *Cybernetic Serendipity: A Walkthrough* (Lee, 2020, p. 79-80).

The hype around artificial intelligence and machine learning in recent years demonstrates how the perceived novelty of a given technology can be used as a marketing tool. This is where Benjamin's ideas about the aura of the individual artwork are turned on its head, in which association with particular technologies may actually impart an aura of its own. Describing machines as authors or artists of highly automated images draws on what Andreas Broeckmann (2019) calls the machine as artist myth. He says:

> **There really is no "machine" outside this narrative, and whenever the word "machine" is uttered, this figure of speech constructs the relationship between human and the technical object within that mythical structure, as binary, antagonistic, and ontologically differentiated.**

This framing poses interactions between humans and technical systems as drawing on far more distinct categories than these indeed are. On the one hand, it can be extremely difficult to differentiate the human from the nonhuman, especially in terms of expressions of agency that are mediated by, through, or with technology. But treating the human and the machine as actively antagonistic against one another imposes an expectation that these may be mutually exclusive. In this passage Broeckmann invokes Martin Burckhardt (2018) on the history of the machine concept, in which he states: "the automatism of any technical system has been seen as both a condition of modern progress and as a betrayal of nature" (p. 41).

Beyond the cultural implications raised by the idea of crediting the apparatus for the production of an image, it also has legal implications in terms of intellectual property rights. The question of whether a machine may be considered an author is significant to determinations of who owns the rights to the outputs of a highly automated system. The fact that many different people may use or adapt the same code, datasets, or prompt inputs makes determining what constitutes an original work, who deserves credit for its creation, and who has the right to make a profit from it fairly murky.

This is especially ambiguous in the recent popularity of image generators that have been trained on datasets of existing artworks from artists who did not consent to the use of their work in such a way.

The idea of machine learning systems as autonomous from human intentionality has serious connotations for highly automated systems' potential to cause harm, as treating a machine learning system as a legally autonomous actor could exculpate the humans who designed, built, and implemented it from responsibility. It also runs a grave risk of masking the many questionable aspects that result from visual applications of machine learning with the presumption that machines are neutral actors. This detracts from what is truly at stake in the power that machine learning systems have to shape — or distort — the aesthetics, discourse, and modalities of image-making.

The emphasis on authorship, whether human or machine, emerges from the view of artists as geniuses or skilled craftspeople, which has been a pervasive narrative in the history of Western art (Elkins, 2015). This perspective posits that the artist imbues their creations with a residue of the creative act, the aura of art in Benjaminian terms. Although discussions of artistic genius are largely unfashionable in current contemporary art contexts, the underlying assumptions it rests on remain influential in discussions and perspectives on visual art in technically-focused contexts surrounding the development of machine learning systems.

The view of the machine artist also tends to draw legitimacy from a belief in a diametric opposition between art and technology. If one subscribes to the idea that art and technology are indeed two distinct forms of practice and knowledge, it then follows that to bridge that gap through demonstrations of artificial creativity or encroachment into other areas presumed to be an exclusively humanistic domain would be a great achievement. For this reason, considerable effort has been devoted to attempts at engineering a machine capable of producing not only images, but even art. The machine artist theme plays out in an abundance of projects that have emerged under the heading of *AI art* (Zylinska, 2020) in recent years, many of which at least are marketed using a similar framing of the presumed dichotomies between human and machine and art and technology.

Recent proposals in the vein of posthumanism (Wolfe, 2009) introduce ambiguities into such polarized understandings of agency and authorship. Zylinska's nonhuman photography, for instance, advocates the need to "expand the human-centric concept of photography by embracing imaging practices from which the human is absent—as its subject, agent, or addressee" (2017, p. 20). She argues that technological developments have given rise to the production of images that incorporate elements that are detached from direct human intervention, intentionality, and interpretation. For example, highly autonomous systems may produce images that do not entail a singular human author, who is responsible for the active creation of an image. A purely nonhuman photography may not be achievable in a strict sense, as it entails cultural constructs that assume the presence of human actors at various stages, for example in the design, set-up, and maintenance of autonomous image-making systems. Furthermore, a nonhuman perspective on photography relies on the cultural constructs of the machine and the image that cannot be extricated by solely shifting the viewpoint away from one that is anthropocentric. As Broeckmann argues, the self is "imbricated with technology" (2019, p. 5) and while this may conflict with intentions to see beyond the strictly human, we are in many ways bound to the situatedness of our own human experience.

ALIGNMENT

The idea of images as being based on or generated from data is now commonplace due to the prevalence of digital media and methodologies that emphasize the production of visualizations based on code. While this is a familiar conception of images, it imposes a particular worldview on how they are to be interpreted, laying the foundation for considering images as a form of data in themselves — the by-product of an analytical process — and it sets the stage for images and data to be rendered interchangeable with one another, as we see in the reciprocal potential for machine learning to be applied to the generation or interpretation of visual media. Images and visual technologies are often posed metaphorically as compatible or even interchangeable with human vision, with the image-making apparatus seen as either a stand-in for the human eye or distanced from the subjectivity of human viewers.

In addition to the creation of images based on rigorous attention to real-world measurements, the incorporation of optical principles and apparatuses facilitated the achievement of greater levels of verisimilitude. This led to the development of new aesthetics, ways of creating images, and, consequently, perspectives on the role played by the technical in mediating between human vision and real-world phenomena. Looking into the incorporation of optical principles into image-making, this chapter considers this positioning of the human point of view in relation to technical methods and apparatuses. Through an examination of the development of linear perspective and an experimental apparatus for the verification of this technique, we consider how visual media may set up and mediate relationships between human visual perception, images, and real-world objects. This leads us to discussion of the role played by technology in visual representations, which, though informed by technical and scientific processes, tools, and principles, are nevertheless subject to variable levels of objectivity.

Various techniques and apparatuses employing optics emerged prior to the development of photographic media in the sense we are familiar with today. Optical methods and apparatuses enabled the development of systematic aesthetic frameworks that are based on the behavior of light, setting up specific relationships between real-world objects and how they are viewed by the human eye. This embedding of optics into the image plane afforded greater correspondence between representation and human vision than techniques solely based on geometry. It also positions the gaze of the viewer in a highly mediated constellation relevant to our investigation of more recent visual paradigms in digital media.

An early experiment in optics offers an illuminating instance of the mediation of visual perception through technical methods and apparatus. Filippo Brunelleschi, who is credited as the first to systematically implement the technique of linear perspective in image-making, also experimented with a method to test the accuracy of an image employing this technique. Artists were likely aware of optics in much earlier periods than the Italian Renaissance, but Brunelleschi is widely recognized as the first to employ this technique systematically in Western art. *Brunelleschi's experiment* (Parronchi, 1964), as it came to be known, involved the design and construction of a tool that could be used to compare an image's visual likeness against a direct view of what it was intended to depict. To achieve this, it was necessary to create a hole in the center of the image in question, and, peering through the picture plane, one could view a reflection of the image for a side-by-side comparison with the scene it is based on.

Other methods and apparatuses developed around the same time as Brunelleschi's experiment involved similar framings of the point of view in relation to representational subjects. Metaphorically framing the point of view, *Alberti's window* (Friedberg 2006) also entailed the development of an apparatus that did this in a more literal sense, using a gridded frame positioned in front of that which should be depicted in observational painting or drawing. This approach imposed linear guides on the artist's field of view, making it easier to gauge spatial relationships within the scene to be represented. The use of similar perspectival devices to that designed by Alberti is documented in two works by Albrecht Dürer, *Draughtsman Making a Perspective Drawing of a Reclining Woman* (c. 1600) and *The Draughtsman of the Lute* (n.d.). In these prints, we see draftsmen peering through a window-like frame to draw a live model and a still life of a lute, respectively. It's also noteworthy that the segmentation of the image that occurs in Alberti's window technique bears a resemblance to the pixel grid of the much later digital image.

Brunelleschi's experimental optics device is especially relevant to the present investigation because it positions relationships between the human point of view and the world in a way that captures aspects of the image as a locus of technically mediated perceptual experience. It aligns the gaze of the viewer with that of the creator of the image, whereby the artist's point of view and that of the audience are assumed to be relative. The device, in this case, is positioned in such a way that it rather poetically mediates the viewer's as well as the artist's perception of both the image and the scene that it depicts. The point of view is thereby split by the apparatus, between a visual representation and the object of representation.

This technique places the image between the human eye, the device, and the world. What one views through this apparatus is thus a comparison between direct perception of the world and perception of the world as mediated through an image that is mediated through technology. This image is thus taken to be a reflection of the perception and intentionality of the human author, as mediated through the apparatuses involved, making this an interesting case for reflection on the technical mediation in image-making.

The idea of visually checking the accuracy of the image with reference to a specific view of the world also sets up specific expectations about the representational accuracy of visual depictions. By employing scientific principles that govern the way the world is perceived by human eyes, images could be made to have a greater level of optical realism. The systematic implementation of optics in visual media through various techniques and apparatuses facilitated the achievement of greater levels of verisimilitude, the appearance of being true or real. That is, by integrating the principles of optics gave images more of a visual correspondence with the real-world objects and scenes they depict than other forms of image-making had previously allowed.

Evidence of this can be found in pre-perspectival images that have a characteristic compositional flatness in comparison to those strategically employing the principles of optics. In such cases, all elements in a composition appear to hover in the same plane rather than visually receding in space. Failed attempts at foreshortening may result in the distortion of proportional relationships between objects and figures or the visual representation of all sides of an object, even though the back side would be obscured from view in direct perception of it. An example in which this kind of visual error is noticeable is the altarpiece from Thuison-les-Abbeville depicting the Ascension, where a person's face looking upward is warped and stretched over a spherical head. Optical media highlighted the fact that unseen parts of objects, such as those hidden behind other objects, could be inferred, rather than visually represented in an image. Imposing a pictorial plane upon representations of the world thereby gave them greater compliance with human optical perception in comparison to other forms of visual presentation.

Long before photography became accepted as an artistic medium in its own right, optical media was explored for the purpose of entertainment. The appropriation of technical and scientific methods and apparatuses in a variety of different applications including in art creates an ongoing tension between visual technologies' aspirations of objectivity and the instability inherent in visual media's reliance on interpretation. The close visual correspondence between optically informed images and direct visual perception contributes to a tendency to associate verisimilitude with objectivity. For example, photography has historically been viewed as producing images that are especially direct, accurate, and realistic in spite of the many instances that demonstrate its capacity to manipulate appearances.

The use of magic lanterns and other precinematic devices in public spectacles became something of an institution in the late 1800s. Less scrupulous lanternists purported to conjure apparitions proving the existence of angels, demons, fairies, and ghosts through their apparatuses. Staged photographs of ghosts, spirits, and demons were also a popular curiosity in early photography. The presentation of phantasmagorias are an especially good example of this, where optical devices were employed to project frightful apparitions, to the delight and horror of audiences. These displays played on the optical realism afforded by devices such as the magic lantern, as well as a suspension of disbelief that often accompanies new technologies. In what came to be known as the "Cottingely Fairies Incident", two girls, Elsie Wright and Frances Griffiths, staged photographic self-portraits in a garden that appeared to be populated by fairies. The apparitions were merely paper cut-outs, but when the images were printed in the newspaper, they are said to have caused public controversy. While it is debatable to what extent such instances are indicative of genuine belief in the photographic illusions portrayed, they do offer a contrast between discourse on visual media at the time and as it stands today.

Before photography, its processes, and its limitations, were widely accessible to non-experts, there was arguably more room to question one's own grasp of what the technology was — or was not — capable of. The tension between the apparent reality and the optical illusion performed in projections of phantasms made magic lantern demonstrations a popular form of entertainment, as well as a lucrative business for swindlers who played up the idea of visually manifesting the spirit world to extract greater profits from uninitiated onlookers.

Similar issues to these have arisen in the hype of machine learning and artificial intelligence, which are often accompanied by misleading claims about their capacity to make accurate predictions about whatever phenomena they are applied to. The tendency of machine learning towards inaccuracy and imbalance is particularly relevant in visual applications, where there is a distinct danger of imposing ethically problematic value judgments on aesthetics. Countless documented instances in which machine learning systems have demonstrated prejudicial tendencies based on factors such as race, gender, sexual orientation, and economic status. It has been duly pointed out that visual applications of machine learning have not only a capacity for error but rather that they are often biased by design.

A common example of the kinds of built-in bias in machine learning systems is the use of unrepresentative datasets that in turn sway their results. For instance, there are several well-known instances in which the fact that many mainstream machine learning datasets are over-representative of white, cis male subjects, causes the systems trained on this data to display bias towards input data fitting those demographics. Joy Buolamwini's *Gender Shades* project (Buolamwini and Gebru, 2018), for example, demonstrates how machine learning systems may discriminate based on race and gender by proving that many systems have trouble recognizing the faces of women and ethnic minorities.

Notions of objectivity in visual representations rely on what Lorraine Daston and Peter Galison (2007) describe as "epistemic virtues" (p. 18), of which they outline three primary forms: truth-to-nature, mechanical objectivity, and trained judgment. The quality of truthfulness to nature hinges on the visual resemblance of an image to a real-world object of representation. The next form they describe is mechanical objectivity, in which instruments and procedures are seen as taking precedence over the subjectivity of the observer of a given phenomenon or the author of an image. In trained judgment, the image does not aspire to visual realism but rather involves a form of visual notation that must be interpreted in a particular, highly informed way. Importantly, Daston and Galison point out, these forms of objectivity are not mutually exclusive:

> **Atlas images — whether reasoned, mechanical, or interpreted — bear the marks of both epistemology and ethos.**
> **[Objectivity] has traced how epistemology and ethos emerged and merged over time and in context, one epistemic virtue often in point-counterpoint opposition to others. But although they may sometimes collide, epistemic virtues do not annihilate one another like rival armies. Rather, they accumulate: truth-to-nature, objectivity, and trained judgment are all still available as ways of image making and ways of life in the sciences today.**
> **(p. 363)**

For an image to be truthful to nature, in Daston and Galison's terms, is one way of registering the accuracy of a visual representation, because it's possible to compare and verify it against the real-world view it is intended to represent. In such a case, the image is understood to mirror the perceptual experience of the one creating the image with that of the eventual viewer. Experience of a real-world, perceivable phenomenon is thereby mediated through the surface of the image, which is itself the product of the tools and processes involved in making the image — that act upon and reinterpret the initial phenomenon.

In the concluding chapter of their exploration of forms of objectivity in scientific atlas images, Daston and Galison describe a progression from representational accuracy to nature towards strategies of presentation, fusing the artifactual with the natural (p. 413). As they describe, atlas images typically aim towards a perfecting of nature, selecting an instance that can serve as an exemplary specimen or model of a given phenomenon. In such a way, these images are therefore singular and specific, while also striving to capture a generalization. This also finds a parallel in images created based on machine learning models, in which the refinement of the model.

Relying on the false assumption that the past is an accurate reflection of the future and basing statistical predictions on existing patterns imposes a troublesome feedback loop that ensures the future will be like the past. This is echoed in the very assumption that all phenomena can be understood through computational methods as in data-based approaches to image production. The interpretive aspects of technology are especially relevant as recent approaches render image and data interchangeable, at least on a practical level. There can be a distinct contrast between the way an image is interpreted by human viewers and the way it is categorized by a machine learning system. Such instances of discrepancy between human and machine interpretation of images are often exploited by adversarial approaches, in which inputs are designed to trigger errors in machine learning systems. The idea that all things are differentiable and countable can contribute to error when applied to things that aren't well grasped through computational means. In many machine learning systems, for example, it is assumed that all images represent something and that they may only represent one thing. Images do not out of necessity have a 1-to-1 relationship with real-world referents, and this is increasingly the case in generated images.

Although an image may be based on data, there is no standard method of mediating between the visual properties of images and the data and processes behind them. In the highly automated and often algorithmically determined image-making techniques that are currently commonplace, there may exist a substantial divide between the visible surface of an image and the processes behind its creation and orchestration. Additionally, applying different methods, models, or tools to the same data can result in vastly different outputs. It can also be extremely difficult to define criteria in order to measure the outcomes of such approaches.

While it is now widely understood that machine learning systems suffer from built-in bias, remediating the problems entailed in these systems is usually not as straightforward as identifying them. The ways in which errors arise are often difficult to diagnose or rectify. Although this has received a great deal of attention in art and the humanities, it remains a highly nuanced and unresolved problem. Merely compensating for the issue of unrepresentative datasets by making the training data more representative of the reality it is intended to represent, as some have proposed, fails to account for the fact that the ethical issues entailed in algorithmic media extend far beyond issues of accuracy. For example, seeking to improve the accuracy of facial-recognition systems in response to their tendency to err in the classification of the faces of women and minorities may run counter to the goal of resisting the forms of control exerted in non-consensual algorithmic surveillance that disproportionately affect precisely the demographics that machine learning datasets are least representative of. Attempting to fix machine learning systems by making them more robust and their training data more representative would also make these systems better at the exertion of problematic, often oppressive, forms of algorithmic control that visual technologies such as biometric surveillance aim towards.

Embedded error and bias is a frequently discussed topic concerning the use of machine learning and artificial intelligence more broadly under the heading of AI ethics. While this is a popular area that has seen significant funding put towards opportunities for artists to intervene with critical perspectives on technology, it may also be seen in the troubling light of simply calling in an artist to solve or rather to whitewash genuine problems within widespread practices by powerful technology corporations. Subversive approaches to algorithmic visual media may be employed in efforts to make machine learning systems less biased or more ethical. But often the nature of such systems leads to a growing sense of futility, and such attempts often result in making machine learning more effective at the questionable practices that had been the intended object of criticism. For instance, by making facial recognition datasets more representative of the actual populations they propose to target, one may actually make machine learning systems better at oppressing, surveilling, and extracting capital from the very people one proposes to represent.

Luciana Parisi (2018) argues that at a foundational level, the internal logic of machine learning imposes a discriminatory form of judgment on that which it is applied to. The mode of discernment in such approaches hinges very literally on discrimination, differentiating one from another. This kind of differential logic is embedded in many ways in fields from philosophy to mathematics, art, and science, yet relies on assumptions that end up producing questionable outcomes. These traditions are informed by ideas about what, and ultimately who, counts, and how that counting is to be carried out. The idea of this being straightforward or neutral relies on the establishment of a highly specific position from which those decisions are then made.

What machine learning images may be verified against is less straightforward than comparing the optical accuracy of photographic images against their referents. Measuring the accuracy of machine learning systems is a complex undertaking for several reasons, including that there are multiple ways for an image to be representative of a computational model. Generated images may appear much like a photographic image, yet they are distanced from the visual verification common to photographic images. We have no way of visually comparing the results against our perception of the object represented in these images and must rely on the precise calibration of technical instruments, the data obtained from them, and their interpretation.

An algorithmically produced image, in this light, may be said to be accurate to the internal rules of the system, but not necessarily bear any relation to specific phenomena in the world. This is duly demonstrated in generative approaches in which images may be produced reliant entirely on algorithmic methods. If one is to analyze the meaning or significance of such generated images with little to no visual referential qualities, instead of being thought of as visualizations of ideas or objects, they may be thought of as manifestations of computation, itself (Carvalhais, 2022, p. 14). This is of consequence because although computational forms of representation may defy expectations of coherent visual referentiality to the real world, they also render real-world referentiality difficult to conclusively rule out. While there is a growing understanding of the potential for manipulation and fabrication using machine learning, establishing the truth value of images grows more difficult as the processes involved become less understandable to non-experts.

Traditional associations of scientific accuracy as a result of the application of the technical processes involved in their production assume that this endows the resulting images with an empirical relation to the world. The representational role of images is itself fairly tenuous, with great variability in the way a visual representation, such as an image, may be said to play proxy for other things such as objects or ideas. While this is a problem that is not exclusive to algorithmic visual media, it reaches new significance as we recognize the difficulty that exists in measuring the outcomes of algorithmic approaches.

Thinking of images as based on data, as data, or as interchangeable with data brings with it a number of complex associations. For example, to think of an image as being based on data involves a quite specific — often technologically- or scientifically-mediated — relation between the image and the world. This opens the possibility to consider an image to be a scientifically accurate visual impression of the world and, furthermore, to consider such a representation to be interchangeable with either the data it represents, that it is composed of, or as a stand-in for the real-world phenomena represented in the image.

Using generative processes to create images and visual content may seem straightforward in itself, but distinguishing "generated images" from those that would be considered non-generative may be ambiguous. For example, in machine learning contexts, differentiating generated images from "natural images" is not only a technical challenge but also a conceptual one. Goodfellow et al. describe as "image(s) that might be captured by a camera in a reasonably ordinary environment, as opposed to a synthetically rendered image, a screenshot of a webpage, etc." (2016, p. 550) While "generated images" in this context designates those that have been produced automatically by computers, natural images, themselves, may also entail a high degree of technical processing, even if they may be based on real-world image data, such as digital photographs.

In a similar fashion, in discriminative machine learning tasks, the distinction between "real" and "fake" images is not an inherent quality of the images but is instead relative or positional within a system. For example, the real images in a machine learning system may be generated, not natural, images, but they are distinguished from the fake images by how they are used, i.e. labeled as such. Artificiality, in this case, has less to do with the attributes of an image than it does with the function or role of the image within the system.

Don Ihde (1979) argues that the mediation of perceptual experience entails a hermeneutic aspect, in which the experience of phenomena is understood as not merely being conveyed, but also altered and interpreted, through media, technology, and technological processes. While a given medium, technology, or approach may enable scientifically accurate outputs to be achieved, these are subject to contextual factors that render that mediation non-neutral.

Appearance is not equivalent to being and the very potential for an image to act as a stand-in for something else speaks to the complexity of this issue. On the one hand, even images with a high degree of verisimilitude are illusory to the extent that they trick the eye into seeing a surface as the thing or things it represents. As Friedrich Kittler notes, paraphrasing Jacques Lacan (1978, p. 103), "art and media are fundamentally about the deception of sensory organs" (1999, p. 38). This is a useful reminder that at their base, the visual qualities of images require us to conceptually translate between two and three dimensions in order to treat the image plane as a representation of the world.

Speaking of an image as being "of" a real-world entity sets up a rather specific, direct, and fixed association between that image and what it visually stands in for. This has led to the idea of optical media as an extension of or stand-in for human vision. The visual accuracy of a photographic image, for example, derives from particular optical relationships that are in large part determined by a combination of the hardware and the procedures involved. This kind of technically mediated referentiality is by no means exclusive to the tradition of photography, nor the aesthetic qualities associated with it. But thinking about images generated using machine learning in terms of this association with themes from the history of photography can be helpful to point out similarities in thinking about referential qualities in media where these relationships may be less directly understandable.

Instead of being thought of as one-to-one representations of objects and ideas, pre-perspectival images often functioned in a more symbolic or allegorical capacity, resulting in different aesthetic priorities than are found, for example, in photographic media. The tendency towards naturalistic representation, which the development of optical media played a part in, signaled a change from images playing a largely symbolic role to images that are based upon the mediation of the perceptual experience of the world through science and technology. Through the examples described in this chapter, the devices of Brunelleschi and Alberti, we see quite directly how technical apparatuses mediate relations between the viewing subject, an object of representation, and the production of an image. Not only does each device mediate the point of view, but its use also aids the viewer in adjusting their image to be more compatible with what is seen. In this way, the technical mediation of human perception comes to modulate the production of images.

There have been various shifts in how optics has been implemented in relation to the viewer, with one-, two-, and three-point perspective and from many devices being binocular towards prioritizing the monocular point of view of photography. Current digital forms of image production may do away with this direct ocular framing of the point of view, but it in many ways may still engage with optical aspects that have been ingrained in aspects of visual technology. Optics may be to some extent negated, bypassed, or ignored, yet many forms of digital media assume the human gaze — and its optical configuration — as a given.

This chapter considered how the implementation of optical principles in image-making impacted visual aesthetics by positioning the viewer's gaze in a specific relationship with the image. From early forms of optical media and Brunelleschi's technique to verify the representational accuracy of images, we then consider parallels between such older forms of visual media and the question of accuracy in machine learning systems. Beyond seeking to make images more compatible with the human eye, technically-mediated forms of visual media offer insights into historical framings of images as visual data about the world, and issues that continue to arise in assessing the accuracy of images.

OPERATION

The widespread use of machines in the performance of visual tasks including not only the production of images but also their interpretation, has altered the structures of visibility entailed in images. While assessments of images have traditionally centered on their visual and material qualities, images are often informed by a range of factors that are not necessarily visually accessible to viewers. Recent theoretical perspectives emphasizing the importance of non-visual aspects of images have been widely influenced by Harun Farocki's concept of the *operative* or *operational image* (2004, p. 12–22), which addressed the estrangement of human, ocular, visual perception from the spatial operations entailed in computer vision. Looking into how the operational image addresses the interplay between the perceptual and the processual, this chapter examines how non-visual aspects of images shape contemporary understandings of the image.

What is visually apparent in an image does not always account for nor correspond with the processes that occur behind or below its visible surface. The *sub-*

face, to use the term coined by Frieder Nake (2008), exists parallel to the perceptible qualities of the image, and in the analysis of images by machines, there may be substantial differences between the visual interpretation of a given image by humans or machines. This surface-subface dichotomy makes it possible, for instance, for images to be produced and interpreted without the direct engagement of human vision nor intentionality. It also allows images and visual processing tasks to be formulated in significantly different ways than those that are intuitively understood by humans. Such situations tend to undermine our grasp of the boundaries between image and non-image, visual and non-visual, and human vision and computer or machine vision. These terms overlap to some extent but in this text, we will give preference to computer vision, which more specifically looks at the extraction of information from imaging, while the latter emphasizes spatial aspects that are contingent on the situatedness of machines.

The divergence between the visual qualities of images and the processes behind them is strikingly apparent in adversarial images, which involve the creation of inputs aimed at triggering errors in machine learning systems (Lee, 2018). These are images that may attack or be misread by a machine learning system, often for the purpose of discovering errors in order to fix them, but as implied by their name, the same approaches could be used with malicious intent. Often approaches to the creation of adversarial images entail exploiting gaps and differences in the way that human visual perception functions in comparison to the processing of visual input by machines. For example, two images that are visually indistinguishable to human viewers may be interpreted in different ways by automated systems. In such an instance, it is apparent that the task of interpreting the images is formulated in a way that prioritizes attributes, criteria, and processes that do not necessarily correspond with the parameters of human visual interpretation. The visual, in this case, is secondary to the operations performed by, on, or in the enactment of images, but it is not excluded from the realm of what images may entail.

Many artists have gravitated towards instances in which machine learning systems fail, with a consistent pursuit of the idea that it is a paradox for machines to behave erratically, to make human-like mistakes, or to be outperformed at simple tasks. This may have a similar basis to the mythologization of artificial intelligence in the sense that there is some satisfaction to be taken in seeking superiority over machines. Algorithmic images are not necessarily non-visual, as is sometimes proposed, but they often leave little for viewers to grasp. This is especially interesting when it occurs in ways where there is much to see, but nothing intelligible to human visual perception. Part of the appeal is that the ways that technologies fail is that situations of error may give access to their inner workings, machine learning being notoriously opaque. Glitch aesthetics play with this by using error as a mode of visualizing processes by interrupting or interfering with them. Error, in this sense, acts as an entry point into what may otherwise be black box, opaque processes.

Redefining the image in terms of the performance of spatial operations by highly automated machines, as opposed to in primarily visual terms, Farocki introduced the concept of the operational image in his influential essay *Phantom Images* (2004). According to Farocki such images are "pictures, made neither to entertain nor to inform", "that do not represent an object, but rather are part of an operation" (p. 17). Using the term more or less interchangeably with the term *operative image,* Farocki argues for a view of images as defined more by the processes they involve than their function as visual depictions, which has traditionally been the primary measure of images. *Phantom Images* acts as a theoretical complement to a series of the artist's practical explorations of how operational images play out in the world. In a series of three video works, entitled *Eye / Machine* (2001–2003), Farocki focuses on situations in which autonomous systems act as analogs for human vision, emphasizing situations employing the use of machine vision.

The idea of the camera acting as a stand-in for the human eye is quite embedded in visual culture, something that is especially visible in "phantom shots" (2004, p. 13) in cinema. Farocki uses an investigation of this cinematic device as a way of leading up to discussion of an estrangement from visual in parallel to the sharing of the point of view with the technical apparatus, as in the spatialized form of navigation performed by drones. Phantom shots use the camera to bring the human point of view to circumstances in which visual processing tasks are not merely taken over by machines but actually displaced by them, for example in contexts where human vision is either unnecessary or incapable. The phantom shot brings about a visual paradox that disrupts the traditional 1-to-1 perspective common in much of photographic media. For example, by visualizing points of view that would be perilous for the human body, such as the underside of a train, plummeting from the sky along with a bomb, or flying through the air like a speeding bullet.

The operational image is important to our understanding of how highly automated, algorithmic processes are engaged in processes of image production, as well as considering what relation this may have, analogous to human vision. Placing emphasis on process is significant because it contributes to a de-visualization of understandings of the image. What is at stake in operational images often has less to do with how they appear than how they behave — how they operate. Images that could be described as operational, may be — and often are — visual on some level, even if in a hypothetical sense, but what is significant here is that the visual is often the least important aspect of operational images.

Adopting a perspective informed by Farocki's operational image allows our focus to shift from the image as a visual representation towards a spatial and processual phenomenon that is performed. Considering how images act on and react to the world as opposed to primarily visual representations echoes the previous chapter's discussion of how significant the processes involved may be to the interpretation of images. To think of an image as a spatial operation, as Farocki's formulation proposes, renders the visual qualities of images secondary to the performance of spatial operations. Images may thereby be thought of as "operational" in the sense that they are not defined solely by how they look or even how they are made, but also how they respond to the world.

Aspects of the operational image and the phenomena it addresses are taken up by numerous other thinkers, with reverberations of Farocki's influence being palpable in several other related theories on the complexities introduced by the automation of visual processing tasks. For example, Trevor Paglen addresses the non-visual aspects of images by referring to the products of machine learning systems as "invisible images" in his 2016 text *Invisible Images* (Your Pictures are Looking at You) and the exhibition *A Study of Invisible Images* (2017). Although descriptive of the capacity of images to exceed the strictly visual is clarifying to some extent, it glosses over the visual qualities that are actually at work in computer vision systems that make them capable of performing sophisticated visual processing tasks such as generating or classifying images.

What is behind the visible surface of an image generated using a machine learning model is the result of an algorithmic reinterpretation of a dataset. Producing new iterations based on countless other images, none of which is to be directly represented in the final product, recalls Jean Baudrillard's *Simulacra and Simulation* (1981), in which he says:

> **Today abstraction is no longer that of the map, the double, the mirror, or the concept. Simulation is no longer that of a territory, a referential being, or a substance. It is the generation by models of a real without origin or reality: a hyperreal.**
> **(p. 1)**

Unlike traditional photographic media, because there is no 1-to-1 referential relationship between the phenomenon and the output, there is no way of determining to what degree generated images are visually representative of their intended subject. There is nothing, no visual reference, against which to compare and judge how well the images capture what they visualize. It is therefore necessary in such cases to rely on the strict calibration and implementation of the instruments involved in collecting the data, in order to ensure the accuracy of the depiction, that is, if generated images are to be understood as representational at all.

Many thinkers have addressed the complex relationship between the visual and the non-visual in images, especially focusing on the role played by highly autonomous machines in mediating visual aesthetics and how the performance of visual processing tasks may occur in ways that do not correspond with human vision. This lack of congruity between human visual perception, images, and the technologies that mediate between them lends itself to discrepancies concerning the primacy of visual or processual aspects in the interpretation of images, whether informed by human perceptual experience and understanding or by algorithmic procedures performed by automated systems. By subverting the primacy of the visual in images, highly automated algorithmic image-making processes leave us with a great deal of difficulty in delineating what an image is, if it is not to be defined by its visual qualities.

Similar efforts to grapple with the ambiguity of the relationship between the visual and the non-visual or processual aspects of highly technical forms of image production have manifested in an abundance of terms that, although insightful, do not offer marked advances forward. As Jussi Parikka points out, merely identifying the non-visual — or invisual (2023) — aspects of visual media does not answer what consequences may be entailed in the removal of the visual from our definition of the image. Images may have non-visual qualities, but if we are to do away with the visual entirely, we are left with a fairly weak definition, as this would allow anything at all to be considered an image. How are we to differentiate, for example, the potentiality of a .jpg, .gif, or .mov file to be displayed in visual form from the visualization of any other kind of file format, or data, for that matter?

"Media are always mixtures of sensory and semiotic elements" (Mitchell, 2015, p. 14), meaning that attempting to draw too stark a dichotomy between the visual and the non-visual may be counterproductive to efforts at understanding algorithmic forms of visual media. Instead of interpreting the non-visual aspects of automated imaging systems to indicate that images are no longer visual, as has been suggested or entertained by numerous theorists and artists working with algorithmic media, computer vision can rather be seen as highlighting differences between various forms of visual interpretation. Framing this as a concern of legibility and visual literacy allows us to move beyond the binaries of the visual and non-visual. And it is once again a reminder that the inclusion of non-visual aspects is not exclusive to recent developments in digital media. What is at stake, instead, is how the relationships between the visual and non-visual components of images, art, or algorithms, taken together, contribute to other things such as conveying an aesthetic experience or conceptual meaning.

The concept of the operational image is relevant to our understanding of algorithmic visual media as it emphasizes the image's enactment in the form of a spatial program — as opposed to being defined primarily in terms of the visual, as has traditionally been the case. This conception of the image supports an understanding of the fact that critical aspects of visual media — artifacts, substrates, and the performance of visual processing tasks — take place outside the realm of visuality. But importantly, as we understand from our examination of this term, what can be thought of as the operational or operative qualities of an image do not rule out its visual qualities, but rather enable us to see what is at stake in a given instance may be processual more so than optical in nature. This is especially tangible in recent developments in which the execution of an image lacks the necessity for direct correspondence with the parameters of human vision and as such, may clash with theoretical attempts at establishing criteria through which to understand them.

REFRACTION

They could no longer contain the many in the one. For them, the link to the multitude of variants could not be held in any single representation, be it ideal, typical, or characteristic. Instead, the most a picture could do was serve as a signpost
(Daston and Galison, 2007, p. 309)

Beyond the direct sense of the plurality entailed in images as a consequence of their technical reproducibility, images are increasingly subject to complex interrelationships between multiple and individual images. A single generated image may be informed by the analysis of countless other images or data that may take a form other than visual media. Such an image is not merely a composite of all the data behind it but rather is the product of a synthesis based on that data. In such a case, the mediation between the many and the one may be governed by technical processes, yet it would be difficult to say what is necessarily represented in the resulting image. For images to be referred to as "data-based" thereby takes on ambiguities that muddle expectations for scientific objectivity in technical image production, and the conditions through which visual knowledge is understood as derived from analytical processes. This chapter looks at approaches to image-making that mediate between individual images and multiple images. Drawing parallels between historical examples and highly technical forms of image generation, we explore how composite image-making strategies lend themselves to particular forms of visual analysis.

Various practices have emerged in which composites of multiple images were made, either overlaying more than one exposure on top of one another or placing them side-by-side in a grid. Looking into historical instances of composite images, we lay the foundations for later examination of parallels between these many-to-one approaches to creating singular images from multiple individual images and the same aspect in machine learning.

Current methods facilitate the production of visualizations based on the analysis of massive amounts of data, visual or otherwise. This may take the form, for example, of generating images using machine learning systems trained on millions of example images, and that are in turn capable of creating innumerable new instances based on statistical models. What is rendered visible in the end product of such a synthesis may not bear a human-intelligible, visual relationship to the images that were input into the system, but instead are entangled through computational processes, structures, and representations. A given image may thereby be understood as bearing the impression of the data-based system it derives from, without that data necessarily being visually present on its surface.

Through different means, compositional strategies that entail the apprehension of multiple images through a singular image offer insight into the more complex processes behind recent algorithmic approaches to image-making. Various experimental photographic techniques in the late 19th and early 20th centuries employed the juxtaposition of multiple images to create composite views that were intended to offer a specific mode of visual analysis. Whether they were produced for pragmatic aims, such as displaying multiple pieces of visual evidence at once, or with purely aesthetic concerns in mind, a number of different instances provide an understanding of how an image may be more than the sum of its parts.

Photography's ability to realistically capture impressions of the world in a matter of seconds quickly earned it a close association with scientific objectivity. Images informed by technical and scientific principles are indeed able to create highly accurate depictions of the world, but this brings with it several ambiguities. For example, photographs may be of something in the sense that they may capture, directly, the play of light off an object in a stable form. But while this has had utility in the development of new ways of visually documenting real-world phenomena, it is heavily reliant on a range of factors beyond the production of the image itself, including, importantly, the mode of analysis an image is subjected to.

By the beginning of the 20th century, photography's potential as a forensic tool was already becoming established. Police started to visually document crime scenes and pieces of evidence, as well as capturing portraits of known or suspected criminals. At the time, it became common practice for police to compile so-called "rogues' galleries," where detectives collected details about criminals, including written testimony from witnesses and increasingly, photographs. Gathering this information was only one part of the problem while organizing it into a usable form was another. Credited for his development of what is now known as a "mugshot":

Police clerk Alphonse Bertillon introduced a rigorous system of classification, or signalment, to help organize archives, a process that included not only quantitative anthropometric measurements of the head, body, and extremities but also qualitative descriptions of the face. Photography's potential for exactitude made it a crucial tool for Bertillon's system, and his portrait parlé — the basis for today's mugshot — posited a powerful analogy between a photographic likeness and the ink fingerprint.
(The Met, 2016)

Bertillon was by no means the originator of the idea of using photography for forensic purposes, but what made his approach especially innovative is that it systematized the way that visual evidence was viewed and interpreted. Allowing multiple views to be compared at once, in addition to incorporating verbal accounts from witnesses, Bertillon's *portrait parlé* technique gave a visual overview of collected evidence related to a case. It also set up a specific analytical framework for these images, for example, by juxtaposing various facial features of potential suspects so they could be easily compared and contrasted. The use of photography in criminal investigations helped to encourage the idea that photographs could act as a scientifically accurate, legally-recognized form of visual evidence. But as James Elkins (1999) highlights, insidious ideas rest behind the idea of analysis "by looking alone" (p. 153), including the imposition of bias in aesthetic judgments, and how visual readings of bodies are often racialized, gendered, or otherwise prejudiced. These themes are familiar within visual applications of machine learning and AI ethics, and they offer a stark reminder of the potential misuse of visual media for nefarious aims, whether intentionally or not.

Even within the early use of photography for the purpose of investigating crimes, there are examples of unscrupulous approaches, such as that of criminologist Cesare Lombroso, whose work has become infamous for its bigotry. Preceding Bertillon in forensic applications of photography by several years, Lombroso pursued ideas encouraged by physiognomy, which sought to make inferences about people's character based on their physical appearance. Like Bertillon, Lombroso, too, created composites of mugshots, but in this case, he attempted to derive generalizable principles based on shared traits among subjects with the aim of establishing visual attributes associated with a look that was presumed to be indicative of a predisposition toward criminality.

Although Lombroso's work is now widely recognized as being based on prejudicial assumptions, it still held some weight at the time. The questionable basis of Lombroso's use of mugshots demonstrates the fact that the ethical dimensions of visual technologies are highly subject to the contexts in which they are applied. This is also the case for the capacity of technologies to develop forms of visual knowledge or evidence. The same instrument or method — the camera, for example — can be used in different ways to deliver wildly different results. And while a given visual technology may have a basis in technical and scientific principles, this is no guarantee of the objectivity of its outcomes.

Arranging pieces of visual evidence on a board or wall has become a familiar cliché in media portrayals of detectives, and related strategies have also long been employed by artists. The use of mood boards enables creative workers to draw from various visual sources including studies or other reference material. Collage techniques traditionally emphasize the juxtaposition of various compositional elements with one another, often using the tension between photographic images to develop conceptual associations. Sequential compositions, such as those exemplified in the layouts of comics or graphic novels, allow a narrative to play out over the course of several frames within a single page. In each case, multiple images coexist in a way that emphasizes temporality, whether simultaneous or progressive.

Explorations of the temporality of still photography can be found in early studies of motion through *chronophotography*. Practitioners of this method investigated photography's capacity to afford new temporalities of seeing than the abilities of human vision alone using various kinds of photographic apparatus. Étienne-Jules Marey and Eadweard Muybridge conducted some of the best-known experiments using this methodology to combine multiple exposures of a single subject over a period of time. Comparing Marey's compositional strategies with those of Muybridge side by side, the diversity of approaches that may be used to capture movement in a single still image becomes apparent. Using long exposures, Marey's chronophotographs, often captured the gestures of walking figures or animals over the course of an interval, layered in a single composition. The fluid, hazy motions of photographs such as *Cheval Blanc Monté* (1886), or the trailing abstraction of *Joinville Soldier Walking* (1883) reveal a distinct compositional strategy from that of Muybridge, whose well-known sequential approach tended to segment movements into discrete frames that are combined in a matrix, as in his studies of animals in motion (1881). Each affords a compound view in which a single panel contains more than the instantaneous snapshot commonly associated with photography today, effectively demonstrating how the temporality of still images may be visualized in different ways.

A curious example of visual analysis of multiple media artifacts simultaneously can be found in Aby Warburg's *Mnemosyne Atlas* (1924). This atlas did not map territory, but rather tried to understand synergies between multiple images at once, using a technique reminiscent of that employed in police investigations. Warburg's expressed aim was "to map the 'afterlife of antiquity,' or how images of great symbolic, intellectual, and emotional power emerge in Western antiquity and then reappear and are reanimated in the art and cosmology of later times and places" (Johnson, 2016). In this pursuit, he created a compositional system for comparing aspects of various images at once. This entailed the production of 63 large, cloth-covered panels, measuring a meter and a half by two meters each, on which visual components could be arranged and rearranged in a way that facilitated the exploration of representational correlations between images. The original panels of the *Mnemosyne Atlas* no longer exist, meaning that scholarship on them is limited to what records remain of them, including photographic and textual documentation and replicas based on these, as in the exhibition *Aby Warburg. Mnemosyne Bilderatlas* at the ZKM: Center for Art and Media, Karlsruhe in 2016.

The experimental methodology employed by Warburg in creating the *Mnemosyne Atlas* did not become an established approach within the humanities but it nevertheless presents a relevant instance in which multiple images are analyzed as parts within a larger whole from the history of visual media prior to the use of digital methods. To call it an atlas implies a form of cultural mapping that was highly contextual and relational. More than strictly focusing on the repetition of aesthetic qualities across time periods and cultures, Warburg sought to understand deeper tendencies behind these manifestations. There is a comparative element in this strategy, not only seeking out commonalities across multiple instances but also looking into what significance may lie in the differences between them.

Although they employ rather diverse techniques, the examples discussed in this chapter each involve the creation of composite images that present visual information in ways that stress the importance of visual interpretation of multiple images at once. There are aesthetic commonalities between them, especially the use of grid-like configurations which can be seen across several of these cases. Far more significant than their visual comparability is that the portrait parlé, the early chronophotographs, and the *Mnemosyne Atlas* each attempt to reveal something that exceeds a singular photographic image. In chronophotography, this entails extending the temporality of the image beyond the straightforward snapshot. What one gathers from looking at either a portrait parlé or panels from the *Mnemosyne Atlas* is comparatively more ephemeral, with visual similarities being only one facet among various clues, pieces of evidence, and knowledge.

In the examples covered in this chapter, new compositions are created through the combination of several individual images to produce a new whole. These kinds of strategies involve a visual synthesis on the part of viewers to take in the one and the many at once. In the case of Bertillon's portrait parlé technique, the compositions are intended for a specific kind of reading and analysis, but one that would be contingent on the particular circumstances of whatever case this methodology is applied to. Although more esoteric in its approach, Warburg's *Mnemosyne Atlas*, too, demonstrates how relative it may be to determine what visual characteristics are salient to understanding tendencies across multiple images. Considering the chronophotographs of Marey and Muybridge from an aesthetic standpoint, the latter are highly segmented, giving a sense of the instantaneity of photography, while the former draw the eye to the fluidity of the movements captured. Each convey temporality and movement in a still image, the *composite* image strategies employed in each case imparting a different form of visual story-telling.

The examples of composite image strategies examined in this chapter demand a particular kind of visual synthesis on behalf of the viewer, requiring not only that several images be apprehended together, but also analyzed. Images such as these especially draw on visual interpretation in a sense that illustrates relevant parallels in the many-to-one approach embodied in many generative machine learning systems. What is especially interesting in the historical approaches covered in this chapter is that instead of concealing the multiple images to be analyzed, as often occurs in machine learning, they are made visible in a way that affords new interpretations of the visual information these compositions are made up of. To call machine learning-generated images *composite* images would be an oversimplification, as they lack the individuation seen in the other examples described as such in this chapter. The composite images examined here are, in contrast, clearly delineated, often with a grid or visual border to mark one from another. But while the term "composite" is not strictly applicable to what goes on in machine learning image production, it does highlight an older form of image synthesis relevant to this investigation, as well as similar aesthetic tendencies that remain present today.

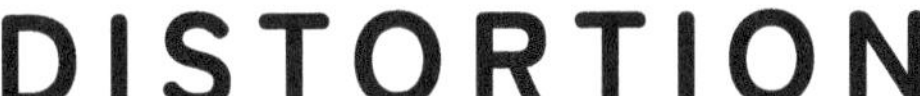

DISTORTION

The increasing tendency for images and art to be informed by algorithmic processes raises new questions about the nature of visual media at the same time as it revives long ongoing debates. While machine learning may have the potential to introduce new modalities into image production, it often replicates, emulates, or expands upon tendencies already present in older paradigms of image-making. Machine learning has proven to have wide-ranging, intricate, and sometimes unpredictable ramifications, such as its inclination towards not only the reiteration but even amplification of embedded biases and ambiguities in the visual and the non-visual aspects of images. As discussed in the previous several chapters, assumptions about the accuracy of visual representation based on the use of technical and scientific methods and instruments of image production have been influential in discourse on visual media, shaping how we think about what we see.

In addition to the aesthetic impact that the increasing use of machine learning has on the production of images, it also influences referential relationships between images, data, and the phenomena they represent. More than merely mirroring the world visually, creating images has the capacity to produce new relationships within the world it represents or interprets. A great deal of variability may exist between real-world phenomena and their visualization through algorithmic methods, making it difficult to necessarily rely on either the visual appearance of an image or the processes behind it as assurance of its truthfulness or accuracy. While visual media is increasingly subject to algorithmic processes that may not necessarily be visualized in a form perceptible to humans, it is also difficult to understand visual media without recourse to the visual.

This book develops an understanding of the cultural backdrop against which recent visual applications of machine learning play out, examining long-running tendencies in discourse around the role of technology in art and image production practices. This seeks to situate emerging uses of visual technologies in relation to a deeper perspective than is commonly applied in recent discussions of machine learning and artificial intelligence. While the products of these approaches may entail novel qualities, modalities, and concepts, many aspects of current discourse on this topic are informed by ideas that emerged in connection with much older forms of visual media. The central examples discussed in this book seek to demonstrate qualities that have given rise to heated debate within art and theory, as well as in public discussions about visual culture, broadly. One such aspect is the formulation of images in written form, which has wide-ranging implications that are difficult to address in a linear fashion, such as following a sequential progression through history.

Allowing images to be made in terms of algorithmic instructions, constraints, and procedures touches on several threads of discourse at once. Doing so affords particular geometric compositional relationships to be encoded in alphanumeric form, enabling the performance of creating an image to be outlined formulaically, with implications for the iterability, seriality, and latency of images thus described. This also allows optical relationships in visual representations to be embedded into methods of image-making, in addition to codifying visual processing tasks in such a way that they may be performed by machines, often detached from the direct control and intentionality of a single, human author.

The development of simple geometric, optical, and mechanically automated methods of image production has wide-ranging implications, ranging from the establishment of criteria for the assessment of the commercial and cultural value of visual artifacts. This is connected to earlier norms around the value of labor invested into images, art, or other products, in which machines have been traditionally seen as distancing human intentionality from whatever is produced. Visual technology thereby shapes not only what we see in images, but also the cultural narratives surrounding the technical mediation of visual perception that occurs through the image.

Recent approaches to the production of images in many ways compound existing visual techniques and technologies into new formulations, allowing multiple visual paradigms to coexist within current visual media. Algorithmic approaches often seek to embed knowledge in the tools that in turn inform that which they are enacted upon, a problem that not only imposes anthropomorphic expectations on machine learning systems but also lends itself to misunderstandings of their outcomes. Indeed, along with the intended content and behavior, we also unwittingly or intentionally embed biases, power relations, and value judgments into these systems as well. This is where fundamental aspects of algorithmic systems and decisions made in the early stages of designing them inform their affordances. The handing over of decision-making to automated algorithmic systems imposes a particular logic on the processes that result from these systems, as well as the outcomes they determine. Far from being neutral or not subject to the subjectivities of humans, the logic of algorithmic interpretation is informed by highly specific values.

From the examples explored in this book, we understand that the design, use, and conceptual framing of image-making techniques each play a role in shaping how, what, and in what terms, we see. Many of the arguments explored here focus on aspects that have historically surrounded judgments concerning the value of images. But perhaps even more consequential to cultural contexts is how this plays out in terms of the forms of subjectivity that highly technical forms of visual media may give rise to. Considering the ideas that have accompanied other paradigms of image production in the past and how some of them continue to resonate through visual media even today, it's essential to reflect upon the values that are ultimately engrained into visual technologies. This is especially important as artists and theorists rush towards what is often a common set of tools, techniques, and algorithms that are largely developed, deployed, and overseen by large corporations in ways that are often opaque, even to their creators.

Aiming to ground recent developments in the production of images using machine learning in relation to the history of art and theories on visual media, this book progresses towards a view of images as not merely representing the world, visually, but rather, acting in and on it. Through examination of relevant examples, paradigm shifts, and ideas from the past, it works upward from simple, analog approaches toward highly complex, digital systems and the use of machine learning. Disrupting the chronological ordering of the history of visual technologies, each chapter cuts across the subject of technical image-making from a different angle, in an effort to develop new perspectives on existing narratives.

Dichotomies frequently arise opposing visual and non-visual, human and machine. This work seeks instead to understand these developments through engagement with the significance of processes to interpretive relationships, both in images, themselves, and in the procedures behind them. Many of the ideas examined in this book conflict with or exist in tension with one another, but this actually taps into central issues that remain open to further theoretical inquiry. Reframing images as processual, temporal, spatial, and relational rather than as objects that are static, material, and above all, visual raises challenges for defining what an image is, as well as delineating what is not an image.

In this sense, the image acts as an interface. It is a site of intersection and interaction between human visual interpretation and intentionality and that expressed by highly automated machines. Algorithms afford particular ways of creating images, and, in turn, of interpreting and reflecting upon visual media. This takes shape in various forms discussed in this book, from structuring images in terms of geometric and optical proportions, allowing the mechanical and digital automation of imaging processes, and even facilitating the generation of new content. These aspects ultimately inform not only how images appear, but also how they behave, and what they mean. And the effect of the use of algorithmic procedures in the creation of images can be seen in the resulting images presenting a very specific, view of the world, informed by technical and scientific methods and apparatuses.

Even in what are considered highly accurate scientific depictions of real-world phenomena, aesthetic decisions are made in how to present the information to human viewers. Like any form of visual technology, the very same approaches, processes, and tools that can be used to create highly accurate scientific models and visualizations based on data can also produce images that have very little basis in reality. And rather than tapping into some kind of aesthetics beyond the human, what machine learning models produce tends to reiterate and further entrench existing patterns.

Machine learning models, which, while in theory may produce any kind of image, in practice often tend to work within a fairly narrow aesthetic range. This is interesting to think about in relation to the co-option of scientific forms of imaging by artists. Using the same tools or techniques that have been developed for scientific purposes to create art throws off some of the framing of expectations for what forms of visual knowledge such technologies may produce. The synthesis of images based on the large-scale analysis of data has the capacity to act on the world, not only translating data into perceptible form but also creating something new in the process. In this, I see algorithmic media's potential to give rise to new and unfamiliar ways of looking at and interacting with the world.

ACKNOWLEDGEMENTS

Many other voices than my own have contributed to this book's realization, whether supporting this work directly or working alongside or ahead of me. With this in mind, I would like to thank some of the people who have been instrumental in this book becoming a reality. Demystifying the cultural implications of algorithms feels as relevant an aim today as it was when I first began working with this topic of research, and it is my sincere wish that this book can contribute to what is already a very active sphere of discourse.

Algorithm, Image, Art is the product of distilling, developing new insights into, and elaborating upon the work of my Ph.D. research, which was originally published in the form of my thesis *Machine Learning and Notions of the Image.* That research was supported with a Ph.D. fellowship from the IT-University of Copenhagen (ITU) (2017–2020) in the Department of Digital Design. Working within such a highly interdisciplinary context challenged me to develop common ground between several different perspectives that converge in the use of algorithms to create images and art.

This book would not have materialized without the support of my husband, Miguel Carvalhais. Thank you for being my sounding board for developing ideas, always challenging me to think in new ways, and encouraging me to keep going.

My family has been incredibly important to the very possibility of conceiving of undertaking something of this nature. I'm so thankful to my dad, Graham Lee, for doing so much to get me to where I am, and for instilling in me the profound importance of education. I want to thank my stepmom, Beth Lee, my sister, Lauren Lee, and my step-grandparents, Carol Woods and the late Harry Woods for supporting me through everything and eagerly asking questions about my work.

Thank you to my editor, Andrew Spano, for guiding me through this process and helping me refine the book into its current form. I am also thankful to Wolfgang Shirmacher for his commitment to cultivating and publishing challenging thinking.

I am especially thankful to those who have advised me, formally or informally during the process of researching and writing this book. Their excellent feedback and encouragement to continue working with this material were essential to my development as a researcher and to the positive outcome of this project. I would like to express my gratitude to my Ph.D. supervisors, Laura Beloff and Sebastian Risi for their guidance during my Ph.D. and beyond. I also want to thank Espen Aarseth, my personnel manager at ITU and unofficial advisor. I am also very appreciative of the feedback of those who were a part of my Ph.D. defense committee, Hans-Joachim Backe, Taina Bucher, and Lev Manovich, as well as to the members of my midway examination committee, Geoff Cox, Miguel Sicart, and Anna Vallgårda. I would like to especially thank Lev Manovich for his enthusiasm for the work and encouragement to publish it in the form of a monograph.

Many friends who are also colleagues in some form have also contributed to making this book possible by supporting me through the process. I want to extend special thanks to all the colleagues whose offices I cried in at some point in the process, an important but often overlooked part of surviving the past 6 years of research. This includes Joleen Blom, Miguel Gonzales, Djordje Grbic, Mads Johansen, Mace Ojala, and Renée Ridgway. My Ph.D. brothers, Jonas Jørgensen, and David Kadish, have been indispensable compatriots and excellent office buddies.

I would like to thank the head of the Digital Design Department, Lone Malmborg, the ITU Ph.D. school, especially Sisse Finken, Julie Lyngsø Berg Jacobsen and Vibe Qvist Mathiasen, and IT Support for their help in making this research possible. The members of the REAL (Robotics, Evolution and Art Lab) research group ended up feeling like an extended family, including Kasper Støy, Andrés Faiña, Mathias Schmidt, Niels Justesen, Frank Veenstra, Rasmus Berg Palm, Mathias Löwe, Stig Anton Nielsen, and Morten Rød Frederiksen. I also want to thank the members of the Department of Digital Design, the Center for Computer Games Research, and MAD: Media Art & Design for making ITU a warm and enjoyable place to work.

BIBLIOGRAPHY

Alberti, Leon Battista. *On Painting (De Pictura).* 1435.
Artnode. *File Room.* 2017. Installation.

Barthes, Roland. "Myth on the Left." In *Mythologies*, 146–49. Paris: Éditions du Seuil, 1957.
Baudrillard, Jean. *Simulacra and Simulation.* Translated by Sheila Faria Glaser. Ann Arbor: The University of Michigan Press, 1981.
Bender, Emily, Timnit Gebru, Angelina McMillian-Major, and Shmargaret Shmitchell. "On the Dangers of Stochastic Parrots: Can Language Models Be Too Big?" In *Conference on Fairness, Accountability, and Transparency (FAcct '21).* Virtual Event, Canada: ACM, New York, NY, USA, 2021.
Benjamin, Walter. "The Work of Art in the Age of Its Technological Reproducibility." In *The Work of Art in the Age of Its Technological Reproducibility and Other Writings on Media*, edited by Michael W Jennings, Brigid Doherty, and Thomas Y Levin. Cambridge: Belknap Press, 1935.
Bianco, Jamie "Skye." "Algorithm." In *Posthuman Glossary*, edited by Rosi Braidotti and Maria Hlavajova, 24. London: Bloomsbury, 2018.
Broeckmann, Andreas. *Machine Art in the Twentieth Century.* Cambridge: MIT Press, 2016.
———. "The Machine as Artist as Myth." Arts 8, no. 1 (2019).
Buolamwini, Joy, and Timnit Gebru. "Gender Shades: Intersectional Accuracy Disparities in Commercial Gender Classification." In *Proceedings of Machine Learning Research*, 81:1–15, 2018.
Burckhardt, Martin. *Philosophie Der Maschine.* Berlin: Matthes & Seitz, 2018.

Cabanne, Pierre. *Dialogues with Marcel Duchamp.* Translated by Ron Padgett. Boston: De Capo Press, 1967.

Carvalhais, Miguel. *Art and Computation.* Rotterdam: V2_ Publishing, 2022.

———. *Artificial Aesthetics: Creative Practices in Computational Art and Design.* Porto: U. Porto Press, 2016.

Cesariano, Cesare. *The Vitruvian Man (L'uomo Vitruviano).* 1521. Illustration.

Crawford, Kate. *Atlas of AI.* New Haven: Yale University Press, 2021.

Cubitt, Sean, Daniel Palmer, and Nathaniel Tkacz. "Digital Light," 16. London: Open Humanities Press, 2015.

Daston, Lorraine, and Peter Galison. *Objectivity.* New York: Zone Books, 2007.

da Vinci, Leonardo. *The Vitruvian Man (L'uomo Vitruviano).* c. 1490. Drawing: metalpoint with wash.

Denson, Shane. *Discorrelated Images.* Durham: Duke University Press, 2020.

Dürer, Albrecht. *Draughtsman Making a Perspective Drawing of a Reclining Woman.* c. 1600. Woodcut.

———. *The Draughtsman of the Lute.* n.d. Woodcut.

Elkins, James. "By Looking Alone." In *Pictures of the Body: Pain and Metamorphosis,* 153–202. Stanford: Stanford University Press, 1999.

———. "The Importance of Skill." In *Master Narratives and Their Discontents,* 123–45. New York: Routledge, 2005.

Farocki, Harun. "Phantom Images." *Public* 29 (2004): 12–22.

Flusser, Vilém. *Towards a Philosophy of Photography.* Translated by Anthony Matthews. London: Reaktion, 1983.

———. *Writings.* Edited by Andreas Ströhl. Translated by Regents of the University of Minnesota. Minneapolis: University of Minnesota Press, 2002.

Friedberg, Anne. *The Virtual Window: From Alberti to Microsoft.* Cambridge: MIT Press, 2006.

Gaboury, Jacob. *Image Objects: An Archaeology of Computer Graphics.* Cambridge: MIT Press, 2021.

Galloway, Alexander. "Are Some Things Unrepresentable?" *Theory, Culture & Society* 28, no. 7–8 (2011): 85–102.

———. "Part I. Photography." In *Uncomputable: Play and Politics in the Long Digital Age,* 15–57. London: Verso, 2021.

Goodfellow, Ian, Yoshua Bengio, and Aaron Courville. *Deep Learning.* Cambridge: MIT Press, 2016.

Hoelzl, Ingrid, and Rémi Marie. "From Softimage to Postimage." *Leonardo* 50, no. 1 (2017): 72–73.

———. *Softimage: Towards a New Theory of the Digital Image.* Bristol: Intellect, 2015.

Ihde, Don. *Postphenomenology: Essays in the Postmodern Context.* Evanston: Northwestern University Press, 1993.

———. *Technics and Praxis: A Philosophy of Technology.* Berlin: Springer, 1979.

Jenkins, Henry. *Convergence Culture: Where Old and New Media Collide.* New York: New York University Press, 2006.

Johnson, Christopher D. "About the Mnemosyne Atlas." The Warburg Institute, 2016.

Johnston, Ron. "Geography." In *Brittanica,* 1999.

Kittler, Friedrich. *Principles of Computer Graphics.* European Graduate School Video Lectures. 2010.

———. *Optical Media.* Cambridge: Polity Press, 1999.

———. "The Finiteness of Algorithms." Presented at the transmediale festival, March 2, 2007.

Lacan, Jacques. *The Four Fundamental Concepts of Psychoanalysis.* Edited by Jacques-Alain Miller. Translated by Alan Sheridan. New York: W. W. Norton & Company, 1978.

Le Corbusier. *Modulor.* 1945. System of anthropometric proportions.

Lee, Rosemary. "Machine Learning and Notions of the Image." PhD Thesis, IT-University of Copenhagen, 2020.

———. "Operative Image: Automation and Autonomy," in "Machine Feeling." *A Peer-Reviewed Journal About (APRJA)* 8, no. 1 (August 2019): 194–202.

———. "Seeing with Machines: Decipherability and Obfuscation in Adversarial Images." In *ISEA 2018: Proceedings of the 24th International Symposium on Electronic Art,* 321–24. Durban: Durban University of Technology, 2018.

LeWitt, Sol. A *Wall Divided Vertically into Fifteen Equal Parts, Each with a Different Line Direction and Colour, and All Combinations.*

1970. Diagram and certificate for wall drawing.
———. "Sentences on Conceptual Art." 0 to 9 5 (January 1969): 4.
Lippard, Lucy. *Six Years: The Dematerialization of the Art Object from 1966 to 1972*. Berkeley: University of California Press, 1973.
Lund, Jacob. "Questionnaire on the Changing Ontology of the Image." *The Nordic Journal of Aesthetics* 30 (July 2021): 6–7.

Mannoni, Laurent. *The Great Art of Light and Shadow: Archaeology of the Cinema*. Exeter: University of Exeter Press, 2000.
Manovich, Lev. "Automating Aesthetics: Artificial Intelligence and Image Culture." *Flash Art International,* October 2017.
———. *The Language of New Media.* Cambridge: MIT Press, 2001.
Marey, Étienne-Jules. *Cheval Blanc Monté*. 1886. Chronophotograph.
———. *Joinville Soldier Walking.* 1883. Geometric chronophotograph.
McLuhan, Marshall. "The Gutenberg Galaxy." In *The Gutenberg Galaxy,* 11–263. Toronto: University of Toronto Press, 1962.
———. *Understanding Media: The Extensions of Man.* Cambridge: MIT Press, 1964.
Mitchell, Melanie. *Artificial Intelligence: A Guide for Thinking Humans.* London: Penguin Books, 2019.
Mitchell, W. J. T. *Image Science***.** Chicago: University of Chicago Press, 2015.
———. *Iconology: Image, Text, Ideology.* Chicago: University of Chicago Press, 1986.
Morton, Timothy. *Hyperobjects: Philosophy and Ecology after the End of the World.* Minneapolis: University of Minnesota Press, 2013.

Muybridge, Eadweard J. *The Attitudes of Animals in Motion*. 1881. Photograph album: iron salt process.

Nake, Frieder. "Surface, Interface, Subface. Three Cases of Interaction and One Concept." In *Paradoxes of Interactivity. Perspectives for Media Theory, Human-Computer Interaction, and Artistic Investigations.* Edited by Uwe Seifert, Jin Hyun Kim, and Anthony Moore. Bielefeld: transcript Verlag, 2008, 92–109.

Nancy, Jean-Luc. *Being Singular-Plural*. Stanford: Stanford University Press, 2000.

Offert, Fabian. "Latent Deep Space: Generative Adversarial Networks (GANs) in the Sciences." *Media+Environment* 3, no. 2 (2021).

Ono, Yoko. *Grapefruit*. Tokyo: Wunternaum Press, 1964.

Paglen, Trevor. *Invisible Images*. 2017. Exhibition.

———. "Invisible Images (Your Pictures Are Looking at You)." *The New Inquiry,* December 2016.

Parikka, Jussi. *Operational Images: From the Visual to the Invisual.* Minneapolis: MIT Press, 2023.

Parisi, Luciana. "Parametricism or Deep Relationality." In *Contagious Architecture: Computation, Aesthetics, and Space,* 102–7. Cambridge, London: MIT Press, 2013.

———. "Critical Theory of Digital Cultures." Goldsmiths University of London, 2018.

Parronchi, Allessandro. "A Reconstruction of Brunelleschi's First Experiment." In *Studi Su La Dolce Prospettiva*. Milan: Aldo Martello Editore, 1964.

Pasquinelli, Matteo, ed. *Alleys of Your Mind: Augmented Intelligence and Its Traumas.* Lüneburg: Meson Press, 2015.
Ptolemy. *Geography (Clavdii Ptholemei Alexandrini Philosophi Cosmographia).* Engraved by Arnold Buckinck and Konrad Sweynheim. c. 150 CE., 1478.
———. *Geography with Twenty-Seven Maps.* Translated by Emanuel Chrysoloras and Jacobus Angelus. Engravings attributed to Francesco di Antonio del Chierico. Florence, c. 150 CE., c. 1475.

Reichardt, Jasia. "Cybernetic Serendipity: A Walkthrough." Presented at C*hance and Control: Art in the Age of Computers,* V&A, October 26, 2018.

Ulricchio, William. "The Algorithmic Turn: Photosynth, Augmented Reality and the State of the Image." *Visual Studies* 26, no. 1 (March 2011): 25–35.
Unknown, *Altarpiece from Thuison-Les-Abbeville,* 1490–1500. Oil painting on panel.

Vitruvius Pollio, Marcus. *The Architecture (De Architectura).* Translated by Morris Hicky Morgan. Cambridge: Harvard University Press.

Warburg, Aby. *Mnemosyne Atlas.* 1924. Installation: 63 panels, cloth, wood, printed photographs.
Weiner, Lawrence. *Statements.* New York: Seth Siegelaub, The Louis Kellner Foundation, 1968.

Wolfe, Cary. *What Is Posthumanism*? Minneapolis: University of Minnesota Press, 2009.

Zeilinger, Martin. *Tactical Entanglements.* Lüneburg: Meson Press, 2021.

Zylinska, Joanna. *AI Art.* London: Open Humanities Press, 2020.

———. *Nonhuman Photography.* Cambridge: MIT Press, 2017.

INDEX

www.ingramcontent.com/pod-product-compliance
Lightning Source LLC
LaVergne TN
LVHW070148120826
845154LV00017B/1

* 9 7 8 1 7 3 7 5 5 9 1 4 6 *